Doing Missions in
Difficult Contexts

ALSO BY PAUL SUNGRO LEE

Disciples of the Nations:
   Multiplying Disciples and Churches in Global Contexts

Missionary Candidate Training:
   Raising Up Third World Missionaries

Doing Missions in Difficult Contexts

Omnidirectional Missions

PAUL SUNGRO LEE

RESOURCE *Publications* · Eugene, Oregon

DOING MISSIONS IN DIFFICULT CONTEXTS
Omnidirectional Missions

Copyright © 2022 Paul Sungro Lee. All rights reserved. Except for brief quotations in critical publications or reviews, no part of this book may be reproduced in any manner without prior written permission from the publisher. Write: Permissions, Wipf and Stock Publishers, 199 W. 8th Ave., Suite 3, Eugene, OR 97401.

Resource Publications
An Imprint of Wipf and Stock Publishers
199 W. 8th Ave., Suite 3
Eugene, OR 97401

www.wipfandstock.com

PAPERBACK ISBN: 978-1-6667-3197-2
HARDCOVER ISBN: 978-1-6667-2512-4
EBOOK ISBN: 978-1-6667-2513-1

03/21/22

This book is composed of edited transcriptions from lectures and study materials prepared by Paul Sungro Lee, PhD, 2022.

All Scripture quotations, unless otherwise indicated are taken from the Holy Bible, New International Version®, NIV®. Copyright © 1973, 1978, 1984, 2011 by Biblica, Inc.™ Used by permission of Zondervan. All rights reserved worldwide. www.zondervan.comThe "NIV" and "New International Version" are trademarks registered in the United States Patent and Trademark Office by Biblica, Inc.™

Scripture quotations marked (KJV) are taken from The Authorized (King James) Version. Rights in the Authorized Version in the United Kingdom are vested in the Crown. Reproduced by permission of the Crown's patentee, Cambridge University Press

Scripture quotations marked (ASV) are taken from the Holy Bible, American Standard Version. In Public Domain.

Scripture quotations marked (NKJV) are taken from the Holy Bible, New King James Version®. Copyright © 1982 by Thomas Nelson. Used by permission. All rights reserved.

Scripture quotations marked (NLT) are taken from the Holy Bible, New Living Translation, copyright ©1996, 2004, 2015 by Tyndale House Foundation. Used by permission of Tyndale House Publishers, Carol Stream, Illinois 60188. All rights reserved.

To Timothy and Titus,
my biological and spiritual sons,
who eminently taught me what it means
to reflect Father God to others
and to make disciples at home.
I'm grateful to father you.

Contents

PART I: SUFFERING NATURE OF MISSION

1. Nobody Likes Suffering — 3
2. Bible's Verdict — 13
3. Rationales of Persecution — 19

PART II: DOING MISSIONS IN DIFFICULT PLACES

4. Mission in Anti-Christian Religious Society — 31
5. Mission in Atheistic Society — 53
6. Mission in Metamodern Society — 60

PART III: DOING MISSIONS IN DIFFICULT CIRCUMSTANCES

7. Mission during Legal Cases — 77
8. Mission in Political Unrest and Natural Calamity — 83
9. Mission during Pandemic — 97

PART IV: TWO FACES OF SUFFERING

10. Another Face of Persecution — 115
11. Mutual Roles of Believers — 123
12. God's Will Be Done on Earth — 147

Bibliography — 169

PART I

Suffering Nature Of Mission

1

Nobody Likes Suffering

RENEWED PERSPECTIVE

As many people do, I love watching football. Each one of my family members is a loyal fan of their favorite teams. We must have watched hundreds of games before, both on the football fields and on TV. We'd normally first check out the lineup of the players on the game day. We used to predict the winner of the day just for fun. Energetic cheers of the crowd, dazzling skills of players, and impressive strategy of coaches top up the list of our reasons to love football. When the scores were made, we'd usually express our excitement with shouts and exclamations. That is the pure beauty of the sport.

Frankly, we didn't care much more than that. However, everything changed when Tim, my son, started to play football. I began to notice things I had never paid attention to before. Somehow my eyes were drawn to an ambulance standing by at a corner of the football field whenever I watched the games ever since. I couldn't help but note that it was always parked backward and was headed toward the exit. I soon learned that the drivers intentionally parked it to hurry to the hospital in case of injury. It was a whole new dimension of watching the football afterward. Why? It could've been my son who might be in the ambulance, not just any player.

I was no longer one of the crowd, but a caring family member of a football player. My perspective was changed.

It became clear to me that day. Even the same should go for my perspective for players of world mission. The way I see and treat the suffering counterpart of the body of Christ had to be renewed. I may not know them well or at all, but my Father does. They're his children. This fact makes them my brothers and sisters in God's grand family. They're not just some statistics remaining unrelated to my tactile interests. They're my family, too. It is my family out there going through harassment and persecution for my Father's business.

I must admit that I was initially hesitant to write this book for several reasons. It was mainly because I thought I lacked the "experience" of suffering and wasn't sure if I'd be qualified to write this book. As far as my memory is stretched, I don't recall myself suffering like those venerable martyrs who went through extreme forms of harassment by imprisonment, torture, and even death for Christ's sake. Though most people may call my missionary experience extensive, it fell short of such dramatic stories. Yet, the Lord has lately laid a special burden in my heart to address this commonly neglected topic. I sensed the global need for partnership with my fellow counterparts in the body of Christ undergoing various aggravations because of their faith.

Besides, I came to conclude that suffering is rather subjective and often internal. The struggle of a church minister over indifferent community responses to the gospel in prosperous post-Christian Europe can be quite overwhelming to him to the point of quitting the ministry. On the other hand, living as a Christian business owner in a Muslim community of the war-torn Gaza Strip certainly invites hassles and threats from the neighbors and risks his safety, needless to say. I don't think any third person has a right to say who is suffering more for Christ. Also, one can't say to the other that he is not suffering enough to bear the marks of Christ (Galatians 6:17). Suffering is deeply internal and to be gauged personally. Even the degree one embodies the hassle and describes it as suffering may differ from individual to individual.

The more I researched and got engaged in the world mission, my concern for the troubled part of Christ's body grew. Eventually, it became a significant part of my daily activities to mindfully pray for them and to seek ways to stand with them. I hope you'll end up with the same takeaway after reading this book. I pray you'll get to feel the urgency and oneness with the suffering players of our Lord's global mission team.

These are not someone else's stories but our own—the stories of a greater family of our God. What you'll read here can happen to you or to the people you know while serving the Lord. With that in mind, this book provides suggestions for difficult missions contexts that were observed and proven effective (and ineffective) over the years as I worked with my coworkers, disciples, and students who served alongside me in numerous corners of the nations, both free and restricted for gospel sharing. Thus, this book is full of biblical exhortations, researches, and anecdotes. In this book, you'll be told genuine stories of how God has worked in the nations through me and my teams, ministering in hostile environments. "Real" scenarios of God's missions in the nations are narrated in the following chapters.

YET SPEAKETH

> . . . He being dead *yet speaketh*. (Hebrews 11:4, KJV, emphasis added)

It was one of those ordinary days in November 2019. An urgent message popped up on my smartphone chat app. A missionary that I knew was just slaughtered by an assailant in southeast Turkey.[1] At first I couldn't believe it because he sent me his periodical prayer letter just a few weeks ago. He was in my class at a missionary training school conducted years ago in South Korea. My heart was aching at this sudden news all the more because of his expectant wife and young child left behind. The second child was born a week after this young missionary passed away.

---

1. International Christian Concern, "Christian Evangelist Murdered in Southeast Turkey."

Two years prior to this incident, I lost my uncle, who was so dear to me. After twenty-plus years of pastoral ministry, he retired and dedicated the rest of his life to traveling to various countries and teaching younger Christian leaders around the globe. I immensely groaned when he passed away due to meningitis inflicted on him during one of his teaching trips to China in 2017.

While I'm aware that the gospel of Christ spreads recurrently at the expense of the sweat and blood of God's people, it vehemently felt more real and firsthand when martyrdom took place to someone I personally knew. It wasn't quite the same as the experiences of martyrdom I'd read about in church history books. Yet, the Bible clearly projected that *everyone who wants to live a godly life in him will be persecuted* (2 Timothy 3:12). The truth is, their sweat and blood did become seeds of world evangelization and their voices of influence still do speak. I, for one, was also motivated by their sacrifices and am penning down this book today even long after they're gone.

"UNNECESSARY" SUFFERINGS?

In my three decades of life as a minister in America, Africa, and Asia, I have never met a person without a problem. You may not recognize it at the first acquaintance, but as you open dialogue and deepen the relationship, it soon becomes obvious and clear. Whether rich or poor, known or unknown, affluent New Yorker or impoverished Sudanese refugee, everyone faces a problem, only different degrees of heat. Yet, there are people who do not mind inviting additional problems by following Christ. Unnecessary sufferings, some might say, at least from a human point of view. However, they choose to risk such challenges simply because they love Jesus more than comfort. They know that the former is permanent but the latter temporary.

In 1998, John Travis coined the term "C-scale," which describes different levels of difficulty for Christian witnesses in Muslim contexts. Although it isn't always clearly compartmentalized as described below, the following table gives us a general idea of the nature of each scale.

C1	Christian in churches radically different from their own culture, where worship is in a language other than their mother tongue.
C2	Same as C1, but worship is in the Christian's mother tongue.
C3	Christians in culturally indigenous Christian churches that avoid cultural forms seen as connected to their religious past (i.e. Islamic, Hindu, Buddhist, etc.).
C4	Christians in culturally indigenous congregations that retain biblically permissible past religious forms (i.e., prostrating in prayer, etc.), investing these with biblical meaning. They may call themselves something other than Christians (i.e. "followers of Jesus"), but do not see themselves as part of their previous religious belief system (i.e. Islamic, Hindu, Buddhist, etc.).
C5	Muslims (Hindus, Buddhists, etc.) who follow Jesus as Lord and Savior in fellowships of like-minded believers within the Muslim (Hindu, Buddhist, etc.) community, continuing to identify culturally and officially as Muslims (Hindus, Buddhists, etc.).
C6	Secret/underground believers.

Table 1. C-Scale (Levels on a scale of Christ-centered communities)[2]

It is quite possible for Christian witnesses in C3 to C6 to experience some forms of hostility and persecution in their attempts to follow Christ. For instance, it was reported in 2000 that six million Muslims annually left Islam in Africa.[3] While the figure was most likely exaggerated for the sake of raising the awareness in Muslim communities against Christian evangelism in Africa, the majority of those converts must have found themselves facing dire situations amid family and community rejections. Though it has been controversial, even the idea of the *insider movement*[4] was created and strategized to suit the needs of Christians undergoing severe persecutions in such communities. Needless to mention, God's people have been challenged with additional suffering as they strived to live in accordance with his will throughout generations.

One of the seminary classes I taught in the past was composed of students from diverse Islamic-country backgrounds. One day,

---

2. Travis, "The C1 to C6 Spectrum," 407–08.

3. Abdallah, "Six Million Muslims Leaving Islam Every Year in Africa."

4. For more exhaustive discussion of the insider movement, see Talman, *Understanding Insider Movements*.

a heated debate was on whether the insider movement was legitimate. A student asked if it would be considered wise to hide his Christian identity to ensure that his moves are not restricted in the Muslim-dominant community in the hope that the freedom might give him more open doors to lead other Muslim neighbors to Christ. As vaguely expected, some assented, while others referred to the movement as a cowardly disguise. The discussion tailed one opinion after another as if water gushed out of a broken dam. After hours of tossing back and forth the opinions which seemed polarized in views, the discussion ended up with two helpful takeaways:

- One should not jump into this sensitive debate without first developing a sense of humility and empathy toward our fellow believers who have to live out Christian witness in such hostile environments.
- The motivation behind the reactions of the oppressed believers greatly matters. It may portray the same outward action but quite different motivation inward, which most humans can't tell. God can, and he will judge the heart.

Rick Brown once responded to Brother Yusuf, one of the preeminent voices of the insider movement, with the following statement:

> For me the important question is not "What works and does not work in Muslim evangelism?" or "Does this have adequate precedent in church history?" For me the important questions are "What is God doing in this community?" and "Am I in harmony with what God is doing or am I resisting it?" We will serve God better if we make it our focus to seek his will for ourselves and for each situation rather than applying the same traditional approach to every situation. God's plan for one fellowship of believers might be different from his plan for another. But if we insist on a traditional model of church for every situation, then we are following the idol of ecclesiastical tradition rather than following the Lord Jesus Christ.[5]

---

5. Corwin, "A Humble Appeal to C5/Insider Movement Muslim Ministry Advocates to Consider Ten Questions," 14.

JESUS' FOREWARNING

This world is turbulent. Jesus lovingly forewarned his followers in John 16:33, "*In this world you will have trouble*. But take heart! I have overcome the world." Open Doors claims that an average of eleven people lost their lives per day for the cause of Christ on this planet in 2019.[6] That number was again similar in 2020—eight people per day.[7] In 2021, it hit the record of thirteen people getting killed every day because of their faith.[8] One in three Christians faces persecution in Asia.[9] For Christians who reside in a society with religious freedom, it may not be easy to grasp the idea of making a living under constant threat and hostility toward Christians. Yet, suffering has been a pivotal part of mission history. Whether we humanly like it or not, the redemptive history of the Christian church begins with suffering in Acts and ends with it in Revelation. Even in the modern missions movements, many reports speak similarly.

When South Pacific missionaries John and Mary Williams arrived on the Polynesian islands in 1817, the place was still dealing with cannibalism, constant wars, and a strong emphasis on magic. Unlike the imagination of some people who picture missionary work in those days as entering idyllic cultures in peace, it was, in fact, very dangerous. John was eventually killed by the hands of cannibals in one of his ministry trips to new islands.[10]

The Middle East and North Africa currently stand out as the prominent hard soils for the gospel penetration despite the fact that the area was a cradle of early Christianity. Many followers of Christ have been, and are, suffering in this part of the world. Early Protestant mission work focused more on developing ancient groups of Christians in those areas to multiply their work. In Egypt, after early attempts to develop the Coptic Church, missionaries came in 1818 but later withdrew. Others came in 1854 but also saw little

---

6. Lowry, "11 Christians Killed Every Day for Their Decision to Follow Jesus."
7. Lowry, "Every Day, 8 Christians Killed for Their Decision to Follow Jesus."
8. Christianity Today, "The 50 Countries Where It's Most Dangerous to Follow Jesus in 2021."
9. Sherwood, "One in Three Christians Face Persecution in Asia, Report Finds."
10. See Prout, *The Life of the Rev. John Williams*.

real success.¹¹ It was hard soil. Henry Martyn, a missionary to Iran, completed the New Testament translation into Persian in 1811. It seemed stagnant for long afterward, however, the seeds have sprouted, and the Iranian Church is the fastest-growing body of Christ in the world today despite apparent persecution.¹² During World War I, Turkey went through political consolidation and massacred 1,500,000 Armenians because of their Christian roots.¹³¹⁴ Today, Armenia is a separate country but in dire poverty. Many Armenian exiles are scattered in Lebanon and around the world.

In the world's most populous nation, China, the cultural revolution (1966–76) resulted in shedding much Christian blood but, at the same time, spurred a significant Protestant church growth. The rejuvenated sinicization policy of Beijing fastened oppression on churches, especially on the house churches and unregistered churches that were loosely operating, deeming Christianity as a desinicization effort. North Korea, where revival once flared in the early twentieth century, has been ruled by communists who have topped the list as the most oppressive country on the Christian witnesses.¹⁵ According to the latest report from the US Commission on International Religious Freedom (USCIRF), North Korea's communist dictatorship has decided to eradicate Christianity. The report confirms that it has been campaigning to annihilate all Christians and Christian groups in North Korea through systematic persecution, including arbitrary arrest and detention, cruel, inhuman and degrading treatment, and torture and execution.¹⁶

Years ago, I was told about several aspects of work in North Korea by my ministry coworkers. It was almost unfeasible to obtain accurate data of underground church membership in North Korea due to extreme secrecy systems that turn even family members over to fierce governmental harassment of Christians.¹⁷ Some

---

11. EBSCO, "Missions and Missionaries Around the World, 1611–1922."

12. See Miller, "Power, Personalities and Politics."

13. Jones, "100 Years Ago, 1.5 Million Christian Armenians Were Systematically Killed. Today, It's Still Not a 'Genocide.'"

14. Morris and Ze'evi, "When Turkey Destroyed Its Christians."

15. Hansen, "Behind Barbed Wire."

16. "Segye seongyo gido jemog 27."

17. Interview with an Evangelical Alliance for Preacher Training/Commission

estimate the North Korean underground church at two hundred to four hundred thousand[18] while others claim over two million strong. However many are out there, we know that they're fellow believers who are suffering under the systematic persecution of Christians by the notorious North Korean regime.

Africa has been depicted as a bloody continent owing to colonization, civil wars, and ethnic cleansings, many of which inflicted harm on and targeted Christians. We see terrorist activities like murder, kidnapping, and rape by radical Islamists across Africa's ice-breaker line, from Kenya to Senegal, where Christian and Muslim cultures collide. Sufferings and persecutions of Jesus' followers are reported from around the globe, from past to present and likely in the future.

As I've been training Christian leaders from scores of the creative access nations, my research on sound and practical methodology to penetrate those difficult areas with the gospel grew widened and deepened. Intrinsically, nobody likes suffering. However, should suffering be one of the "necessary" costs to be paid to follow the King of Kings and Lord of Lords, it is worthwhile to face it wisely and prudently. That is the intention of this book—to elaborate on practical and biblical models of mission for difficult contexts, including in the creative access regions (CAR).

What is God doing in this reflection of ongoing suffering? We should be able to read the sign of our times in the context of suffering and injustice around the world. So often, we're directed to one dimension of missions driven by traditional missionary methodology rather than open to the possible multi-sidedness of the mission. It is now high time to consider multidirectional methodologies as the world gets exposed to greater diversity and complexity. It is now time to go beyond the one-dimensional narrative of reaching the world for Christ. We must understand that mission works in such difficult areas have a multidimensional spectrum to face and real challenges to deal with. After all, we serve an omnipotent and omniscient God. Then, our mission strategy should be also omnidirectional. There may not be "one-size-fits-all" textbook answers

---

missionary to China, October 15, 2016.

18. Open Doors. "North Korea."

for every possible scenario. This book does not intend to provide a solution or answer to each and every challenging situation but invite the readers to a school of thought to contemplate biblically and tangibly on the viable obstacles by sharing missionary experiences and missiological research that my missions coworkers and I have encountered for the past quarter-century.

Prepared minds will convincingly equip us to act soberly and prudently without perplexity and be attentive to the voice and leading of the Holy Spirit. Taking the Great Commission seriously demands risk: suffering, sacrifice, and even life at times. It is my prayer that the Holy Spirit will remind you of what you read in this book in case he allows you to end up in those inevitable opportunities to suffer for Christ's name in one way or another.

2

Bible's Verdict

HEAD AND BODY IN SUFFERING

John Terry defines missiology as the science of missions which studies theology, history, concomitant philosophies of missions, and their strategic implementation in a given cultural setting.[1] While we'll be doing in this book exactly what missiology does, chapters 2 and 3 are dedicated to discussing the theology and philosophy of suffering in mission.

This world is a wounded world with some form of Christian suffering and persecution found almost everywhere. Simply put, the body of Christ suffers because the head suffered. Timothy Tennent speaks of Christ as the suffering servant by expounding on the book of Isaiah in his *Invitation to World Missions*.[2] Suffering Christ begets suffering Christians.

> Very truly I tell you, no servant is greater than his master,
> nor is a messenger greater than the one who sent him.
> (John 13:16)

Suffering nature is innate in the body of Christ, as it was in Christ himself from the origin and depth of eternity. As Christ's

---

1. Terry et al., *Missiology*, 8.
2. Tennent, *Invitation to World Missions*, 116–19.

followers seek to live godly lives in compliance with his teaching, suffering might as well meet them on the way. Since the fall of Adam, this world has increasingly witnessed wounds of suffering servants globally and regionally. Misuse of power and vulnerability of the underprivileged often caused segregation, discrimination, and inequality in most parts of human societies. In the modern era, nationalism, postmodernism, and sequential metamodernism backfired as countertrends, yet are still a threat to the body of Christ on her path to pursue righteousness.

We're in the mission of God in its diversity and continuity. However, we affirm that this world is not well. Take for instance the 1994 Rwanda genocide. Eight hundred thousand lives perished in a tribal clash in the name of ethnic cleansing. Human slaughter on both large and small scales still takes place in Africa. Human lives, especially those of the poor and marginalized, aren't valued in the beloved continent. There are no murders, only regrettable deaths. I've witnessed this firsthand during my sixteen years of life in Africa. Africa, for one, has been a dire victim of corrupted human hearts. Like the rest of the world, Africa has two faces. Next to most of the affluent communities are found overpopulated slums and impoverished ghettos. The poor work for the rich neighborhood, and they ironically coexist. Some enlightened leaders give impetus to introduce entrepreneurship in emerging African economies, but the number of those good Samaritans seems to be never enough.

One of the greatest threats to social development is the issue of corruption. In his book *Truth and Transformation: A Manifesto for Ailing Nations*, Vishal Mangalwadi describes that corruption is rooted in covetousness and the unbiblical idea; it is magnified by materialistic consumerism; it is facilitated by moral relativism; it thrives apart from fear of God. He further goes on and suggests that these areas should be dealt with and be touched through the culture of the cross.[3] It is the root problem of all the problems in the world—sin—with which Jesus came to deal through his substitutionary death on the cross. Only in Christ, the solution for every devastating effect of sin, including human corruption, begins to unfold.

---

3. See Mangalwadi, *Truth and Transformation*, Appendix 1.

When I was ministering in different parts of Africa, I remember some of the policemen who routinely pulled over cars on the roads to ask for bribes. Once pulled over, they'd normally "make up" any traffic violations, leading drivers to get away by giving bribes. My wife Eunice and I were easier targets to them, being foreigners. Corrupt policemen even took us to police stations when we constantly refused to give in. After many years of repeating the same scenario while driving, I almost felt paranoid each time I saw traffic police on the road. It may not appear on the missions textbook or even be considered as suffering for Christ, but the threat is very real.

In the Philippines, both Eunice and I occasionally fell sick because we could not sleep for several nights due to the loud karaoke singing of the neighborhood. Culturally, Filipinos love music and cherish mirth. It isn't difficult to meet fiesta parades in various towns. However, some neighbors went too far and sang outdoor day and night. Most houses in the Philippines were built without soundproofing, and you can hear every noise the next house makes. In respect of their cultural protocols, we talked with our neighbors, called the community association, and even asked the community head for help, but all were in vain because the neighbor calmed down for a few days but came back with the same scenario all over. We ultimately had to get ear plugs and use them to sleep those loathsome nights.

There is an old saying: "Many small drops make a big flood." Accumulative and repetitive discomfort can affect a missionary's health in the long term. It is certainly different from the emotional fear and possible physical assault I sensed from Chinese policemen who raided a church in the middle of my preaching in China. You may not feel a direct hit from such minor degrees of irritations, yet those kinds of sufferings are also very genuine when repeated for years. Suffering exists in different forms wherever and whenever God's people endeavor to follow the call of Christ.

Owing to the self-centeredness of crooked mankind, vulnerable ones are isolated, trapped, and ill-prioritized in the injustice of the social system. In the midst of it all, the body of Christ is called to share the Master's love just as he did during the unfair Roman

Empire's rule in his days of flesh on earth. Jesus still weeps over the injustice of this corrupt world as he wept over Jerusalem before his triumphant entry. Our expression of Christ's love in the missions of God may be imperfect. Nonetheless, it is still the job of the church to present five loaves of bread and two fish to the vulnerable ones whether it produces a miracle or not.

SUFFERINGS AT GOD'S SERVICE

When an American missionary was killed in 2019 in his attempt to make contact with the Sentinelese tribe in India, the body of Christ reacted with different opinions and roused controversy regarding the legitimacy of his missionary methodology.[4] While his grief-stricken family members unquestionably deserve our condolences for their loss, some Christians began to seriously consider that the best missionary methodology might not be just sharing the gospel, but sharing it with respect for other cultures. Certainly, it may not be easy to figure out how its practice looks like in various mission fields. This notion stirs us to funnel through a valuable and critical thinking process during the pre-field preparation.[5] Only history will tell of the meaning of his sacrifice in the years to come.

When the early church believers faced persecution, thousands chose death rather than the denial of their faith. Many preferred to burn at the stake for their love for the Master most of whom had never seen. Christ honored their sacrifice, and their blood became the seed of the church, as Tertullian put it.[6] For us who live two millennia away from the birth of the Christian church, this history alone encourages us in the most meaningful way. If millions—not one or two—including both learned and unlearned, rich and poor, men and women, Jews and non-Jews, and many more in the history chose *Christ with death* over *no Christ with life*, wouldn't the cause of Christ be something of absolute worth? What could be more valuable than their own life? Why did those people follow Christ at the risk of gruesome deaths unless they assumed Christ was bigger

---

4. Lamb, "Art of Dying Well," 43.
5. Austen, "From Jim Elliot to John Allen Chau."
6. Hanks, *Seventy Great Christians*; Boer, *A Short History of the Early Church*, 21–22.

than their name and prestige? If Jesus was that worthy for them, what does it mean to me today? These are legitimate thoughts that certainly deserve our time for contemplation and resolution.

It is also notable that almost every one of the Twelve whom the Lord must have dearly loved was martyred for him. If Jesus loved them so, wouldn't he have to keep them from slaughter and give them wealth and health so that they might propagate the message for as long as they lived happily ever after? History tells us differently. This is why the prosperity gospel can't soundly explain the glory of martyrdom.

Having a Korean heritage, I used to wonder why God allowed the first Korean Christians during the Joseon Dynasty to face severe persecution—at first from the royal palace who deemed Christian activity a threat to national security and later from Japanese colonialists who worked to wipe out Korean culture, language, and history. Christians suffer the severest form of oppression in North Korea under a totalitarian communist regime even today. One could've thought, "Wouldn't God need to protect those Korean believers from the brutality of Japanese subjugation and communist invasion since they've finally opened a door to the gospel after living as heathens for so long?" From a human perspective, it is a valid question. Yet, the reality is, a great many Christians have suffered and died under Japanese and communist rule since Christianity first set foot on Korean soil. They've matchlessly spoken out to their successors about how worth it following Christ is. Their sacrifices were never in vain. The modern phenomena of South Korean church growth undoubtedly owe them for the solid foundation laid by their blood, sweat, and tears.

Consider this thought for a moment. Both exhausted, a pregnant teenage mother and a puzzled father traveled across a Roman colony. They were the very tools the almighty God used to prepare for the Savior's incarnation into the world. The Father did not provide for them a five-star hotel room nor the finest birthing suite to welcome his incarnate Son into this world, but in a trivial manger in the animals' stable was he laid. It wasn't because the Father couldn't afford to do so. Jesus' missionary incarnation sought out for the blessing of people he came to serve, not his own comfort.

This humble perspective may keep a missionary in a prayerful mode and prudent actions in challenging situations he faces on the mission field.

As Christopher Wright stated rightfully, our mission (if it is biblically informed and validated) is God's own mission in his own history.[7] In 2 Corinthians 8:1–5, Paul talks about the Macedonian church who overflew with joy during severe trials and extreme poverty they faced. Trials and sufferings couldn't shake Macedonian believers because things of this world weren't their purpose. Those things were simply tools to attain their eternal purpose. The secret of their heavenly lifestyle on earth was subject to their recognition of who they belonged to, not what belonged to them. Every one of us will also face trials and sufferings at some point, and just like the Macedonians, we must decide who or what we will trust when we face our own trials. Recognizing and choosing the former will lead us to a wise life that leaves a shining legacy like the brightness of the heavens and the stars (Daniel 12:3).

---

7. Wright, *The Mission of God: Unlocking the Bible's Grand Narrative*, 23.

3

Rationales of Persecution

BIBLICAL THEOLOGY OF RISK AND SUFFERING

What is the biblical basis of suffering? What makes it legitimate? It falls under one of life's hardest questions first because "suffering" is rather a subjective term. The degree of what is perceived as suffering may vary per individual. What is tolerable to one can be draconian to others and considered as suffering. Another reason it's hard to answer that is perhaps the loathsome nature of the term. It naturally seems detestable to most of us when it hits us. We simply do not want to think or talk about that.

Suffering is real, but why doesn't God put an end to all the sufferings, miseries, and persecutions in this world right at this moment? Mankind has wrestled with this dilemma for so long. The Bible, however, does give the following three logics for why sufferings exist in our world. This world is dominantly a fallen world, from human hearts to every level of nature and society. Deeply saturated by the effects of sin, the fallen world touches every aspect of our life and, in so doing, produces pain and suffering. Furthermore, God-given free will has been repetitively misused by people to choose evil over justice, and it has continuously invited sufferings to come and stay with us. The other logic is connected with the devil's plot to derange with deception and iniquity this beautiful world God has made. Suffering typically increases when people exercise apathy over evil. Persecution of Christians today has more to do with global economics and politics than it has to do with Christian beliefs, as in the early church.[1] Yet, the highlight of our history shines out around the hand of God that keeps reaching out through the cross of Christ to heal this broken world marred by human flaws.

Then, where is God amid the rampant sufferings of mankind? Steven Chalke tackles this difficult question with the following propositions: (1) God can't take care of them because he isn't omnipotent in the presence of overwhelming problems of mankind. (2) God is omnipotent but indifferent to the suffering of mankind so he wouldn't intervene. (3) God is loving and all-powerful but sometimes allows and uses the suffering for the long-term (rather, eternal-term) benefits of mankind.[2] We may never fully comprehend precisely why suffering exists or why God allows suffering to us while living on this side of eternity. Hitherto the Bible's standpoint supports the third proposition as the initial answer to this centuries-old question.

BIBLICAL MISSIOLOGY OF RISK AND SUFFERING

When Eunice and I were serving as missionaries in Kenya, one day a call reached us from Seattle. A church elder wanted his wayward son to come and stay with us in Nairobi for a couple of months so that he might shape up by tasting "suffering" life on the mission field. Gently yet profoundly, we refused the idea largely because we didn't feel peace in our hearts after praying about it. Besides, our experience told us that life on mission fields is challenging enough even for the best missionary candidates, let alone a young man who was unwillingly forced by his parents to go try it. We were afraid it'd turn out to be disadvantageous both to the boy (and his parents) and to our Kenyan coworkers. It was our creed that someone who wasn't approved at home would not be much different on a mission field.

1. Ilo, "Pandemic, Persecution and Poverty."
2. Chalke and Hansford, *The Truth about Suffering*.

Suffering in God's work is not to be entertained lightly. I've heard some missionaries and missionary candidates heroically mentioning Christian suffering as some sort of extra virtue, epic, or decoration. Far be it from the reality of suffering! We're talking about the life of someone's son, daughter, husband, wife, father, or mother. Instead, our preparation and prayer should be put in order for a more realistic and effective strategy by articulating and dealing with its elements, just in case it falls on us according to God's all-knowing plan. We should overcome the temptation of hedonism and self-compliance[3] and consider how our attitudes and responses toward suffering may influence those around us. We only need to suffer for what God has allowed us to. All Christians, including cross-cultural missionaries, are God's representatives to someone and, therefore, are public figures in that sense. They need to be mindful of how their reactions to suffering and persecution matter to the public and influence others for Christ.

Every strategic trajectory of Christian missions has a clear rationale about (1) what it is like, (2) why it is done that way, and (3) how it is done. Knowing the types of suffering that our missionaries and missionary candidates may get into can readily prepare them. Research of the most up-to-date field situation and analysis of factual field data must be made in advance. Areas of danger and risk should be consulted and cautioned against early. For example, it wouldn't be generally wise for a single lady missionary to walk alone in a part of town with a dead-end alley in the day or night. Car windows should be rolled up with doors locked at the stop signs when a missionary passes through an area rampant with pickpockets. Common sense should be applied. There are sufferings caused not necessarily by God's will but rather by man's recklessness and negligence. Such troubles can be largely prevented with our prudence. We ought to know exactly what we've signed up for and what possible sufferings may await us on our mission fields.

We also need to be aware of why suffering and persecution are likely on our way while doing missions. Much of "why" is discussed in part I of this book. The Bible apparently endorses them, as previously discussed in chapter 2. The head (Christ) suffered for us, and

---

3. Lee, *Disciples of the Nations*, 128–29.

so does his body now. Sometimes, sufferings are mysteriously used by God to work for the good of those who love him (Romans 8:28).

Now here comes the rationale concerning the "how" of missionary suffering. For instance, we need to remember that it's not easy to measure the accurate number of converts anywhere in the world because it isn't always feasible to define signs of conversion—decision cards, baptisms, church membership may not exactly represent the number of converts, although they provide us some hints of the information.[4] Similarly to that account, there is a fine line between martyrdom, accident, and the outcome of the reckless act. The line is pretty ambiguous. However, the biblical definition of martyrdom is certainly connected to the *voluntary* enduring of suffering (to the point of death) on account of Christ. Martyrs had their choices not to suffer (to the point of death) but chose to do so out of their love for Jesus. If they chose to denounce Christ, they could have been freed from the imminent suffering (to the point of death).

Above all, martyrdom is a gift bestowed by God, not a domain that man can handpick. In the early church, a difference between martyr and confessor was distinctively made. Because not everyone who proclaimed Christ's lordship at trial suffered the death penalty, the terms "martyr" and "confessor" were coined to distinguish the two.[5] Besides, motivation greatly matters in martyrdom. One's motivation is more of an internal issue, which is unfortunately difficult for the third person to discern. Only God and the suffering servant himself would know the heart of the person at risk. However, there are ways others may still be able to tell whether his persecution and heart were legitimate.

LEGITIMACY OF RISK AND SUFFERING

Back in Kenya, I remember a meeting of several field directors representing different mission agencies gathered together to discuss an incident of a certain missionary whose behavior became a matter of some concern among missionaries. The missionary just

---

4. Miller and Johnstone, "Believers in Christ from a Muslim Background," 5–7.
5. Bixler, "How the Early Church Viewed Martyrs."

came on the mission field in his golden years after retirement. It was during the month of Ramadan, the Islamic fasting period. Presumably urged by his passion to proclaim the gospel, he went to a Muslim-dominant part of the slum in Nairobi with a sound system and engaged in street preaching in front of the largest mosque in the area. His message was concise and repetitive: "Jesus is the Truth and Muhammad a liar, so believe in Jesus and you will be saved." About half an hour later, a group of enraged Muslims gushed out of the mosque and began to stone him. Badly injured, the missionary took selfies at the spot and later sent them to his donors. He boastfully claimed that he was persecuted for preaching God's word.

Field directors went to see him at the hospital to comfort him and also exhort him, but this missionary bluntly refused to listen to their advice. He persisted in his offensive method for months and eventually left the town when he realized he couldn't continue with the same scheme any longer. Afterward, Christians not only could not engage in public street preaching for years but also multiple restrictions were put on their outreach activities by the area chief to prevent religious clashes in a particular section of the community.

Church history verifies that (1) *means* and (2) *fruition* of missionary work do matter. Those two usually tell whether the suffering and persecution a missionary went through were legitimate. The means may be immediately noticeable, but again the heart and motivation of the missionary are unlikely to be detected at the spot. I've seen missionaries and mission groups giving into the pressure of offering bribery to government officials to speed up the process of their field operations. While it may be debatable to define the term "bribery,"[6] the universal principle still stands. The corrupt seed will produce corrupt fruit someday.

> Be not deceived; God is not mocked: for whatsoever a man soweth, that shall he also reap. For he that soweth unto his own flesh shall of the flesh reap corruption; but he that soweth unto the Spirit shall of the Spirit reap eternal life. (Galatians 6:7–8, ASV)

---

6. See Koteskey, *Missionaries and bribes*, 20–33.

It may take longer, possibly years, for the fruition to show up. For example, after John Williams was martyred in Polynesia, his local disciples kept visiting the new islands and evangelizing the area. History tells us that the London Missionary Society, Williams's sending agency, also went on and operated seven missionary ships in the Pacific to share the gospel in honor of his name.[7] The seed of blood John Williams sowed ultimately stirred up the hearts of his successors and raised future missionary forces after he was gone.

Robert Thomas from Wales traveled to Korea (Joseon back then) with stacks of the Korean Bibles on an American warship in 1866. Korean crowds who deemed Thomas as one of the foreign invaders attacked him and beheaded him as soon as he put his foot on Korean soil. Years passed by. Interestingly, the pages of a Bible which Thomas brought to Korea were used as wallpaper in somebody's home. They were accidentally read by a man who happened to stay in the house and ended up giving his heart to Christ. Through this man, and others like him, the foundation of the church of Korea was subsequently laid. The blood of Thomas was eventually used by God to build his church on a sure foundation of martyrdom. Some might have doubted if Thomas's death was worthwhile, since he only lasted hours before he was slain by locals.

I repeatedly warn my ministerial students to be careful not to get trapped by the three most deceptive motivations for missions: (1) self-glorification (missions as adventure), (2) self-righteousness (missions as earning God's approval), and (3) self-entertainment (missions as hedonism).[8] They're not only dangerous for the missionary's overall wellbeing but also degrading to the very people he goes to serve. Kyle Donn points out the danger of stylish and "sexy" Christianity by listing notable distinctions with which so-called radical Christians love to stand out among other Christians. They sensationally practice a smart-casual-attire, simple-living, guitar-playing, coffee-drinking, justice-loving, and short-term-missions-tripping Christianity. Doing a mission looks "cool" to them, but its suffering ingredient hardly does. Early church believers were

---

7. Wingfield, "Ship's Bell, United Kingdom," 127–29.
8. Lee, *Disciples of the Nations*, 128–29.

heavily engaged in cross-cultural missions not for stylish spiritual caviar but their survival amid persecution that broke out after Stephen's martyrdom. There was no budget, no ministry plan, and no hand sanitizer in their missionary work—not that I'm trying to demean their usefulness. They were on the run for their life while doing a mission. Donn further states that our culture has taken the biblical faith over and sold it for cheap after giving it a make-over.[9] Real missions involve paying the bills, washing dishes, parenting children, cultivating marriage, and doing other dirty work on most days in the field. Disciples are raised and souls saved in the middle of such "ordinary" daily life.

Biblical suffering and persecution are never attractive to stylish Christianity. A good percentage of the students I've been teaching came from the CAR, most of whom have either experienced themselves or witnessed someone go through family disownment, physical assault, homelessness, moneylessness, injustice, and community hatred all because of their faith in Jesus. To most of them, Christianity is not a matter of style. It is a matter of life and death.

RATIONALES OF CHRISTIAN RISK AND SUFFERING

A certain mission organization launched a citywide parade with Christian messages written on banners and marched through the streets of a major city in the Middle East. Hundreds of short-term missionaries flew in from overseas to participate in the event. It was during the socially sensitive period of Ramadan. They were claiming to have a "Jericho march" to pray for and redeem the lost city for Christ. There was no prior consultation with field missionaries who had been serving years in this difficult area with various indirect mission approaches for pre-evangelism. Field missionaries had a hard time coping with the aftermath when this mission group has left. The group made much public display and fundraising media content for those who financed them and prayed for this event from back home. Many residents, including the field missionaries, however, condemned the event.

9. Donn, "The Dangerous Allure of 'Sexy Christianity.'"

Aggressive and offensive mission approaches may be mysteriously used by God at times to accomplish his sovereign purposes. Time will tell by the fruit whether such approaches were of God indeed. Meanwhile, strategic approaches are cordially recommended and crucially required as we move closer toward completion of the Great Commission and get nearer to our Lord's return. With ISIS and other militant religious organizations on the horizon with a counterattack on the Christian mission groups, strategic missionary work and missions training are in greater demand. Thorough pre-field research will always be helpful. Selfless cooperation between front-line mission (those who go) and behind-line mission (those who send) will merit successful field work, effective missionary member care, and proper stewardship of mission funds.[10]

Christ, the Messiah, came into this world to sacrifice his life for mankind. We, Christians, share this nature on earth while representing his heavenly kingdom and witnessing his love for us. Both English terms "martyr" and "witness" share the same original Greek word: μάρτυς. The word is used more than thirty times throughout the New Testament. This plainly shows us that a martyr is someone who bears testimony (to the point of death). That is the kind of lifestyle Jesus wants us to pursue whether we're based in the free world or the gospel-restricted world. It is this *living sacrifice* disposition that Paul urges us to adapt to our day-to-day conduct (Romans 12:1). We're called to tell this message to others both near and far, both with and without words, in our 24/7 in the context in which Christ situated us: that Jesus is our Savior and Lord.

For well over two thousand years, the Bible-believing Christians worldwide celebrated the Lord's Supper (or the Communion) and remembered what Jesus has done for them. Think about this for a moment. Our communion with Christ is knitted with his sacrificial love for us. Participating in his broken body and shed blood draws us closer to uniting with our Lord. Jesus' body was broken and his blood shed for the world. We're his body. Given to the world for Christ's service, this innate nature of the body of Christ revolves around the sacrificial offering of ourselves to the

---

10. Lee, *Missionary Candidate Training*, 39.

Lord and others. That kind of sacrifice usually magnets the world to the Lord.

> . . . But if you suffer for doing good and you endure it, this is commendable before God. To this you were called, because Christ suffered for you, leaving you an example, that you should follow in his steps. (1 Peter 2:20–21)

In this context, the content of martyrdom should be focused more on one's lifestyle than his death. It would not make much sense for someone to live debaucherously all his life and suddenly choose a heroic death for Christ in his last breath. Dying well is preceded by living well first. It begins with living faithfully for Christ before dying for him. One who experienced Christ's irresistible love finds a sufficient rationale for the suffering and persecution he may face. After all, I'm the reason that Jesus came and gave his life. He then becomes my indisputable reason for suffering, if inevitable. Christ who loved me becomes enough reason for me to endure any suffering and persecution.

> We are hard pressed on every side, but not crushed; perplexed, but not in despair; persecuted, but not abandoned; struck down, but not destroyed. We always carry around in our body the death of Jesus, so that the life of Jesus may also be revealed in our body. (2 Corinthians 4:8–10)

PART II

Doing Missions in Difficult Places

4

Mission in Anti-Christian Religious Society

STORIES OF THE PERSECUTED WORLD

Mission is the work of the Holy Spirit. He is in charge and leading it throughout history. We've witnessed time and again that he works mysteriously and unexpectedly every so often. He always gets his job done and knows what he is doing. These are a series of testimonies and anecdotes of such marvelous deeds he is doing among the nations.

The latest advancement of online communication made it possible for us to reach deeper into the ministry of our disciples who serve in nations that are restricted to gospel sharing and hostile to Christian presence. For decades, we've tirelessly worked in Africa and Asia to raise Christian leaders. Forty-eight of the fifty most persecuted global churches are found in those two continents. In 2021, top fifty most difficult countries to follow Christ included: Pakistan (#5), India (#10), Sudan (#13), China (#17), Myanmar (#18), and Vietnam (#19).[1] Eunice and I have been reaching out to those challenging countries through leadership training and church planting. Indeed, they still do not guarantee the liberty of

---

1. Open Doors. "2021 World Watch List Report."

worship for Christians, albeit far more developed economically than in the past.

Pastor "Q" and Brother "T" serving in Vietnam are two such examples of Christian leaders committed to discipling young professionals in ominous environments.[2] Pastor "N" and his wife have been in our mentoring group while undergoing ministerial training in the Philippines before they returned to India. Upon graduation, they decided to go to Hindu-dominated regions of Northern India instead of the Christian regions of South India where they originated from. Their devoted work continues to bear the fruits of new church plants and leadership training in hostile communities. Several Burmese students are currently enrolled in my online classes, and Myanmar is paralyzed by an ongoing military coup d'état, rousing protests, and subsequential violence against citizens. The nation is in dire unrest. My heart is constantly reaching out to them in prayer for their safety and ministry. An over-95-percent Muslim-dominated nation,[3] Pakistan stands out as one of the countries where women and children are neglected and mistreated. Mrs. "N," who Eunice taught the importance of children's ministry during her seminary training in the Philippines, has gone back to Pakistan and is now reaching out to the least of the society through children's ministry among the poor. At the onset of the coronavirus outbreak, the work of the Evangelical Alliance for Preacher Training/Commission (EAPTC) has been moving more secretively due to increased regulation and exhaustive surveillance imposed on churches and pastors by the Chinese government in the name of community quarantines. All internet content is monitored in China. It is interiorly difficult for someone who marks as "Christian" on his identification card to find decent jobs except low-paying (often degrading) jobs in most of the countries mentioned above.[4]

Investigation of Amnesty International revealed that Pegasus, the spyware created by NSO Group, the Israeli security firm, has been extensively used to target journalists, human rights activists,

---

2. For security purposes, I use initials in this book to mention certain names of individuals and places.

3. Operation World, "Pray for: Pakistan."

4. Open Doors, "Vietnam."

businessmen, and politicians around the world. When this spyware penetrates a cell phone or computer, all personal information can be retrieved and the targets are constantly monitored and controlled. This means that not only freedom of speech and human rights but also freedom of religion can be violated. Rwanda, Mexico, Morocco, Bahrain, Saudi Arabia, Azerbaijan, India, Kazakhstan, Togo, and the United Arab Emirates are known to have purchased the spyware. Some of these countries are authoritarian countries with potential persecutions imposed on Christians. It is now possible for their governments to strengthen the surveillance and control of Christians through IT and other online tools. There's a critical and increasing need to work wisely in online communication with our fellow believers in those regions.

Picture 1. Church in Pakistan[5]

It is our sheer privilege to equip those suffering servants around the world through the sacrificial prayer and giving of dedicated mission partners. With sincere empathy and agonized intercession for what our coworkers and disciples go through each day, we're happy to be their hands and feet to serve them with training and encouragement. It's extremely rewarding to see them share Christ's hope and love where his light is still dim.

---

5. Image by Paul Sungro Lee.

FUTURE CHALLENGES OF THE GLOBAL CHURCH

The primary reason they suffer is that they chose to follow Jesus. There's still a great multitude of such faithful witnesses in the world. Issues of natural disasters or epidemics usually take a political turn in many places and intensify persecutions toward Christians. Nevertheless, the amazing truth is, churches grow and believers mature in the persecuted world amid ongoing challenges. We witness the refined churches and sanctified ministers of Christ shining through the dark tunnels. Our fellow believers in the persecuted churches covet prayers, as Paul asked the church of Colossae to do the same:

> And pray for us, too, that God may open a door for our message, so that we may proclaim the mystery of Christ, for which I am in chains. (Colossians 4:3)

One day I received a message from Pastor "M," a former student of mine who now serves in Pakistan with outreaches and church plants to unreached areas of this Muslim-dominated country. Before he and his ministry team embarked on another outreach trip to various towns in Pakistan, M specifically asked us to intercede for them with the prayer of Acts 4:29:

> Now, Lord, consider their threats and enable your servants to speak your word with great boldness.

He reminded me that the first Christians didn't pray for physical protection, comfortable life, fortune, fame, health, and wealth, but God's will, God's plans, and God's mission to unfold in their lives. They'd rather see God empowering them to boldly speak of Jesus with grace, courage, and power amid persecution and pressure. This pastor portrays the mark of a true witness by choosing God's will over personal comfort. Persecution may limit direct ministry access, but *missio Deo* (missions of God) has never stopped. God's kingdom keeps marching on and gets rooted in the nations. In history, hostility against Christians or churches has been categorized as (1) anger, (2) antagonism, (3) agitation, and (4) aggression.[6] As you can see in the below analysis on the

---

6. Wells, *Incarnational Mission*, 100–101.

mechanism of the persecuted world, persecution engines act as a catalyst for various interests of men in power to gain the security of absolute power.

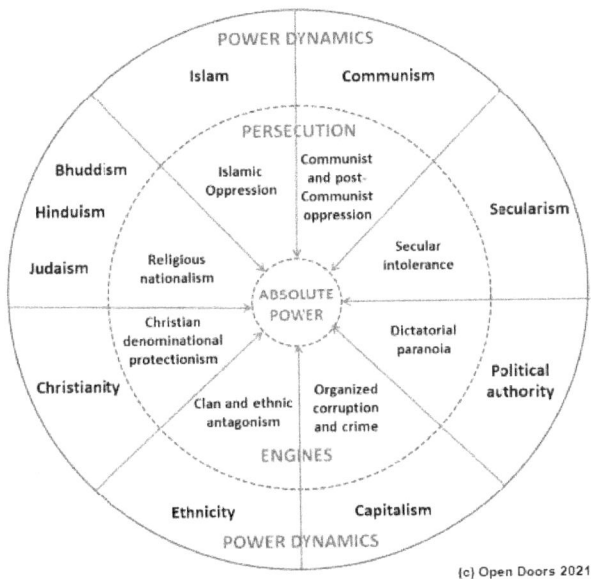

Figure 1. Persecution Engines[7]

Patrick Johnstone predicts that the global church of the twenty-first century will be more than likely facing a continuous share of suffering to those who live for Christ just as in the twentieth century. In the early twenty-first century, the global church suffered the heaviest discrimination and persecution in regions like Saudi Arabia, North Korea, the Maldives, Western Sahara, Iran, Afghanistan, and Somalia, to top the seven on the chart.[8] Coincidentally, most Christian growth and missions are projected to come from underdeveloped and troubled regions of the globe.[9] This sets a trajectory that the future challenge of the global church will generally fall under the category of (1) an anti-Christian religious society (i.e.

---

7. Open Doors International, "Complete World Watch List Methodology," 13. Used with permission.

8. Johnstone, *The Future of the Global Church: History, Trends and Possibilities*, 96–97.

9. Ho, "When Leaders Drink Tea Together," 2.

Islamic, Buddhist, Hindu, etc.), or (2) atheistic society (i.e. communistic), or (3) secularized metamodern (post-postmodern) society. Eighty-five percent of the least-reached peoples of the world reside in either Muslim or Hindu societies. They're also known as the Frontier People Groups (FPG) who have less than 0.1 percent Christian populations, most of whom are under some form of persecution. We do live in the time of unprecedented persecution and martyrdom of Christians.[10] More Christians have been persecuted in the past few years than at any other time in history, and the number of martyrs is expected to rise to one million by 2025.[11]

Kenneth Shreve, who ministered in the CAR for years, describes the area as characterized by non-Christian dominant religion, no recognized indigenous church, and no missionary activity allowed. However, the emergence of the Global South, the internet, and new missionary vision and strategy shaped the mission to that part of the world.[12] While it'll be certainly challenging to minister in such regions, my experience and research show that vibrant small groups or house churches can minister effectively in most of those difficult places and contexts of missions. As a matter of fact, the church was meeting in the houses in her original format. That is how the early church was able to not only survive but thrive under the fierce persecution of the Roman Empire.

The worldwide COVID-led lockdowns reminded the body of Christ that the church is not a building but a people. The conceptual definition of the church has gone through a drastic change and even distortion in history. There is an explanation for why most people perceive a church as a place (building) rather than as people (believers) today.[13] Before the time of Constantine, the early church found its nests mostly in small domestic spaces of someone's house. Even Jesus and his disciples utilized domestic houses for ministry. Those house churches were clearly their mission strategy to reach surrounding regions.[14] It was rightfully a "house" church. After the

---

10. Lewis, "Clarifying the Remaining Frontier Mission Task."

11. Johnson et al., "Christianity 2018: More African Christians and Counting Martyrs," 25.

12. Shreve, *Partnership Theology in Creative Access Regions*, 155.

13. Manaloto, *Let the Church Meet in Your House!*, 164.

14. Manaloto, *Let the Church Meet in Your House!*, 164.

freedom to worship was granted, a house church setting gradually evolved to a basilical setting, likened to a mobile tabernacle structure, evolving to a permanent temple structure. Some of those magnificent architectures undoubtedly conveyed the message of God's glory and honor. Yet the downside was that worshippers began to enjoy and became comfortable with this development. Nevertheless, we still find this key missionary strategy of the early church at work for the gospel-restricted areas. The original church form penetrated the communities even after two thousand years passed by.

MISSION AND ANTI-CHRISTIAN SOCIETY

A gospel worker targeting ministry in anti-Christian society ought to consider the distinctive features it has, especially concerning the hostility toward Christianity.[15] He needs to first immerse himself in the target culture and people. Identifying the problem and need in the community can be considered for the next step. His contribution to the betterment of the community can slowly earn public acknowledgment and open a way to connect with the neighbors in due time at the very point of their needs. As he meets and relates with people, God may lead him to start with a handful of people whom he can disciple to be future leaders and followers of Jesus who can also disciple others. They should be pointed to the biblical mandate of discipling others and multiplying the discipleship in the community.

The task of missions gets burdensome and difficult without acquiring enough knowledge of the culture and people. Having adequate knowledge (i.e. of people's history, beliefs, religion, practices, priorities, challenges, and mindset) helps the gospel worker better acquainted with his target society. Detailed research and thorough knowledge of the community pave a path for transformation. Reaching people in a hostile, gospel-restricted community is not easy, since they're occupied with beliefs, practices, and attitudes which repel Christian workers. Christian witnesses are called

---

15. Yancey, *Hostile Environment: Understanding and Responding to Anti-Christian Bias*, 85.

to live out the implications of the gospel as they engage their neighbors in a multi-religious world.[16] The incarnational mission is extra crucial for anyone who gets involved in mission and evangelism in the areas like the CAR. Some creative and practical approaches are suggested in the following field researches that were conducted by me and my students who regularly minister there.

In Muslim Society

Though somewhat controversial with the means to measure the Muslim population worldwide, more than fifty countries are still considered Muslim-majority nations.[17] Many Islamic states prohibit the conversion of their citizens to Christianity either by civil law or customary law.[18] There are certainly more tolerant Muslim societies than others, but, in a general sense, it is not wise for a Christian to openly share the gospel in many Muslim societies due to communal or individual oppressions. They could exist both in explicit and implicit forms.

The Taliban's recent takeover of power after the US troop withdrawal agreement put Afghan believers in manifold dangers. The believers who boldly professed their Christian identity to the public by changing their names from Muslim names to Christian names were quickly targeted by the Taliban for elimination. When the Taliban came into power, they collected data from the registration office to pursue them. They even slaughtered the government officials who helped register their Christian names on the record, I was told by a pastor who was engaged in a relief aid mission for Afghan refugees.

In such explicit settings, one may need to find indirect ways to share the gospel, like medical outreaches or small community projects. A number of my Pakistani students are engaged in running food relief camps, which regularly open opportunities to share Christ's love with the Muslim community and to pray for their beneficiaries. Sharing and caring can go hand in hand. However, sound interpersonal relationships with the target group must

---

16. Brockman and Habito, *The Gospel among Religions*, 152.
17. Farrokh, "Perceptions of Muslim Identity," 117.
18. See Darwish, *Cruel and Usual Punishment*.

be intentionally cultivated—with the community leaders, if possible—for these programs to penetrate. The process may take years, and, along the way, sharing the contextualized gospel is in order at any given chance.

A testimony of how Christ has personally changed your life can stir the Muslim neighbor's soul to resonate with a real power to transform lives. Jesus is but a mere prophet in Islamic theology; therefore, Christ's divinity ought to be articulated at opportune times. Most Muslims struggle with the uncertain destination of their afterlife, believing that only a fair amount of good works may grant them access to heaven. Christ's free gift of passage to heaven through his sacrificial death can literally turn out to be the "good" news to those whose spiritual thirst hasn't been quenched in Islam. In so doing, we must keep trusting in the power of the shared word and work of the Holy Spirit, prompting those who have ears to hear (Matthew 11:15; Mark 4:9; 4:23; Revelation 2:7; 2:11; 2:17; 2:29; 3:6; 3:13; 3:22; 13:9).

We should keep in mind that Christians are looked down upon in Islamic culture since we're considered the enemies of God and distorters of his written message. Islamic culture perceives Christians (especially those in the West) to have misunderstood and misrepresented God. Muslims are disgusted at the West, those who tolerate promiscuity, abortions, disrespect for parents, and neglect of the elderly.[19] Heavily influenced by Western media, entertainment, and Hollywood, many Muslims mistakenly associate Christians with the West and consider them interchangeable in their perception of Christianity.

Accustomed to a circular communication style, which doesn't directly speak out about their discomfort, many Muslims would not outwardly express their feelings. Linear communication style, which swiftly gets to the point, may not be in the loop of Muslim communities.[20] People have a social disposition to be welcoming on the outside, but inside they're more or less occupied with prejudice. In Muslim communities, identifying and meeting the felt needs of people is one strategic approach rather than presenting the gospel straight away.

19. Pikkert, "Protestant Missionaries to the Middle East," 287–88.
20. Lewis, *When Cultures Collide*, 30.

A gospel worker might as well find Qur'anic grounds upon which he can build a bridge with his Muslim neighbor. Such grounds include (1) Isa (Jesus in Arabic) as a prophet, (2) the supernatural birth of Isa, (3) Abraham and the sacrifice (despite the difference of Isaac versus Ishmael being the sacrifice), and (4) the miracles performed by Isa. One may utilize those grounds and depend on the Lord to speak through him the appropriate words at the right timings. However, he should be careful not to diverge into a theological quarrel out of his witnessing to Muslims, because Islam forbids Trinitarianism, incarnational beliefs and the worship of Christ.[21] It will lead him nowhere. These grounds are but mere triggers to open a dialogue.

Some missionaries debate over the anecdotal case studies of using the Qur'an as a path to Jesus (also known as the camel method), which has raised not a little dispute in the missiological circle.[22] While I have no doubt it'll be effective to some Muslims, I tend to point out that the root issue goes far deeper than the application of the camel method to bridge with the Muslim community. In history, Christians left a severe scar in the Muslim community, and the scar has to be dealt with beneath the surface of just using the familiar Qur'an verses to win Muslims.[23] Ten different failed crusades, both on large and small scales, have historically left a blood mark in the hearts of the Muslims. On one occasion, even child soldiers were recruited and involved in the war. Those crusades are considered by most Muslims as barbaric Frankish invasions in the name of a holy war.[24] To make matters worse, seven eighths of the entire Muslim world was colonized by the so-called Christian nations by the end of World War II.[25] Had we obeyed the Great Commission and loved the Muslims just as Christ commanded us, we would not see extreme and fanatic Islamic terrorists as known as today.

Perhaps we need to echo the heartfelt prayer of Ramon Llull, the venerable missionary to Arabs who served during the time of

---

21. See Farrokh, "Pursuing Integrated Identity in Christ in Ministry to Muslims."

22. See Oppenheimer, "A Dispute on Using the Koran as a Path to Jesus."

23. Nevertheless, a list of Qu'ran verses to address Jesus and the gospel is well discussed in chapter 7 of my previous book, Lee, *Missionary Candidate Training*, 29–38.

24. Sullivan, "Why Muslims See the Crusades So Differently from Christians."

25. Open Doors. "Brother Andrew Webcast."

the crusades when crusaders were making horrible and fatal mistakes of misrepresenting Christ to people of the Middle East:

> It is my belief, O Christ, that the conquest of the Holy Land should be accomplished in no other way than as Thou and Thy apostles undertook to accomplish it—by love, by prayer, by tears, and by the offering up of their own lives.[26]

Marks of true Christians can still crack the rock-hardened hearts of Muslims as they demonstrate Christ's arm and reflect his unconditional love. When Christianity returns to its core method of biblical propaganda—the personal conviction of the gospel—it will regain godly influence in the society, including any religious society where there is nothing but dead rules and regulations. Even Jesus was supra-religious. In the anti-Christian religious society, Christians can and should exercise more politics of humility with respect for diversity rather than an antagonistic attitude toward other religions.[27]

Lastly, people in the Islamic world are reportedly desperate to be set free from the bondage of magic and curse. Our Lord Jesus is able and willing to liberate them and use his servants as instruments of divine freedom. It floors leading Muslims to Christ in the end. Many Muslim-background Christians (MBCs) or Christians of Muslim background (CMBs) today testify that they're former recipients of such manifestation of Christ's supernatural power at work.

In Hindu Society

> I am sending you out like sheep among wolves. Therefore be as shrewd as snakes and as innocent as doves. (Matthew 10:16)

If you're following Christ in a Hindu-dominant region, there is a reason God put you where you are. He wants to fulfill his purpose

---

26. Mathieson, "Ramon Llull."
27. Casper, "The Best Advice on Engaging Muslims, from Arab Evangelical Scholars."

through you there. It takes wisdom to be prudent and shrewd to do the missions right in the Hindu community while keeping the gentleness of Christ. There's a grand opportunity for sharing the gospel in Hindu communities, even as the imminent challenges are great.

While a large Hindu representation is likewise discovered in its neighboring countries of Nepal and Bangladesh, India is solely the largest Hindu country, with over 70 percent of the national population subscribed to that religion. The evangelical Christian population comprises only 2 to 3 percent of India.[28] This stat directly contributes to impending threats to the Christians and Christian activities in the nation. Pastors, evangelists, and mission workers both local and expatriate face various types of challenges. Yet God's work hasn't halted in the Hindu nations. The more persecution came about, the more vibrant church growth has taken place in past years. Romans 5:20 affirms that where sin abounded, grace did much more abound.

India is a vastly diverse nation with different ethnicities. While most regions of the country fall under Hinduism and Islam, there's a smaller percentage of Christian regions spread mainly in the south. Many of my Indian students from those Christian regions reach out to other regions, particularly the north, where Hinduism is dominant and often violent. They're actively involved in gospel sharing, community development, and leadership training. There are numerous regions in India where Christian workers are molested and the churches burned by the Hindu mob.

Narendra Modi, the Prime Minister of India, assumed his office in 2014. Modi belongs to the BJP (Bharatiya Janata Party) political party, the main Hindutva (Hindu nationalist) political party in India. The party promotes national Hinduization and has provided Hindu extremists a social platform to pester non-Hindus since he came in power. Persecution of Christians has intensified, including the re-Hinduization agenda of the Dalits group, about 70 percent of whom are Christians.[29] Dalits, meaning the "untouchables," are the lowest Indian caste hierarchy under Brahmins (priests), Kshatriyas (warriors), Vaisyas (herders, farmers, merchants, and craftspeople),

---

28. Operation World, "Pray for: India."
29. Selvamani, "Dalits, Dalit Christians and Dalit Christian Liberation Theology."

and Sudras (farm workers, servants, and laborers).[30] Dalits make up about 16 percent of the total population of India. They mainly deal with carcasses, leather repairs, street sweeping, and conventional toilet manure disposal. Some of them work as peasant farmers, slashers, and farm servants. When a Dalit converts to Christianity, he has to pay several prices. If Christians from Dalit backgrounds give up their Hindu-based caste identity, they must give up benefits such as free college tuition, job opportunities, and government subsidies. They're the most vulnerable and marginalized group in society and obviously have become a target of radical Hindu groups. Even the operations of foreign missions that have connections with the local Dalit Christians have been hindered by the government. The Indian government's aggressive stance to defend Hinduism and oppress other faiths has created the unspoken indulgence for religious violence and bolstered up Hindu persecutors. Deeply rooted in India, religious and social discrimination against the Dalits is one dire issue that demands a biblical answer. Also, Christians from Dalit backgrounds can use our prayers to keep their faith in the face of discrimination and oppression. These are some of the case studies which my students have encountered in their outreaches for Hindu communities.

In several Tamil communities of India and Sri Lanka, contextualized gospel sharing was practiced through the means of Pattimandram (the art of debating). Rich in vocabulary, the Tamil language is one of the oldest languages in the world, possibly older than Sanskrit. Pattimandram is a part of the rich cultural heritage for Tamils, one of the oldest ethnic groups in India and the neighboring countries. The Pattimandram tradition provides a platform for two teams of people to debate on various thoughts and life values and encourages listeners to brainstorm about them. There are usually two or more members in each team who debate on both the supporting and opposing arguments on the given topic. Speakers often cite Tamil poets, literature, and narratives to build their arguments. The audience enjoys listening to their speeches and often considers it a treat to ponder their talks on various topics of life, values, and tradition. The moderator normally gives a final verdict

30. Pruthi, *Indian Caste System*, 5–34.

after hearing the speeches from both teams. The concept of Pattimandram usually draws people to think about life and its meaning and arouses them to seek questions and answers about them. The events are frequently aired on TV and other mass media and thus can cause a ripple effect. Tamils regularly find their cultural literary works interesting and relevant to their life, including non-Hinduistic ideas. Should a Christian messenger learn to present the contextualized gospel message without using "Christianese," Pattimandram can be one powerful way to plant the seeds of the gospel in the Tamil communities.

Meanwhile, first things should come first. Relationship building with people, preferably with community leaders, is recommended and is to be prioritized. There's another case study of my Indian student who primarily made an effort to build relationships with other families in his community. After the relationship building with the parents of the community, he initiated a sports ministry with the kids in town. A weekly Bible study class was gradually introduced and added. People need to be transformed first for the culture to be transformed. For this reason, I'd encourage a Christian missionary to participate in community occasions and festivals, of course with some degree of cautious self-restriction in the involvement, because not all such practices may be godly or tolerable. Only a few Christians go visit their Hindu neighbors and their social functions but still expect them to come to their Christmas celebrations and other similar events. Interfaith communication channels are seldom established. Unnecessary barriers between Christians and Hindus are erected by Christians themselves at times. Jesus called us to be the salt and light of this world. Unless the salt is applied to the food and the light in the darkness, they wouldn't do much good. It is now high time for the believers to break the barrier and, in turn, do the missions right to reach out to the people God has given to us by sharing the gospel strategically and winning the Hindus for Christ.

Please remember that most converts from Hindu backgrounds came to Christ because of their attraction to his power and love manifested through the selfless ministry of their Christian friends. Building a long-term bridge with your Hindu friends and presenting the gospel through narrative storytelling of the Bible and your personal testimony in opportune times will pave a way to lead them to the true Savior of the Hindus. After all, Jesus holds the power and love to touch millions of our Hindu neighbors and free them from powerless and loveless Hindu gods.

When many parts of India were severely affected by the COVID-19 outbreak, local churches have gained people's trust and welcomed when they opened up their worship facilities as community care centers for people of diverse faith backgrounds. The crisis turned into an opportunity to love their neighbors. Such testimonies opened doors for the gospel in the areas where Christian discrimination rapidly grew due to the anti-conversion act promoted by the BJP as well as violence multiplied by extremists.[31] Love can, in the end, warm the hearts of Hindu society and open doors for the mission.

In Buddhist Society

In reality, many Christians who have been converted from a Buddhist background live as strangers in their own lands. Being a Christian in Buddhist society is a process rather than an event for Thai believers.[32] While some Buddhism-dominant societies are tolerant to Christian witnessing activities, many of them do exhibit communal or individual oppression just as in Muslim society and Hindu society. Vigorous Buddhist society possesses a developing sense of hostility toward Christianity and Western propaganda. Our research shows that the mission in the Buddhist community must intentionally differentiate between the gospel and Western culture. Typical Buddhists consider Jesus a foreign god, specifically that of the West. Conversion to Christianity, therefore, can be deemed as a desertion of one's own cultural heritage and defection to westernization. Critical contextualization of the gospel message must proceed to build a bridge with the Buddhist community. Culture shapes inward worldviews and outward behaviors of the

---

31. "Segye seongyo gido jemog 27."
32. Blumenstock, "Living as Strangers in a Familiar Land."

people. Some of the Buddhist worldviews which stumble on the gospel message are intertwined with the following concepts:

First, Christianity is a Western religion and shouldn't be imposed on the Asian concept. Western beliefs, including Christianity, are unwelcome to many Asian Buddhists with discriminatory attitudes. Without a solid foundation of friendship and contextualization, the gospel message may not penetrate deeper. Our walk and talk should match for them to sense the genuineness of our message.

Second, we must be aware of the polite behaviors of our Buddhist friends. When people say yes occasionally, it is just about the portrayal of their respect and politeness. Missionaries need to see their wording and behavior through a missiological lens. It may not be easy for a missionary with the Western worldview to fully comprehend this part of characteristics of his Asian Buddhist friends without an intercultural attitude. We need an insight into the biases of the Western worldview and the way the biases teach those of us who are products of Western culture to think and to act. North American Christian workers need to be mindful of and develop an anthropological practice with cross-culturally relevant applications.

Third, the notion of a good deed in the animistic, Hindu-Buddhist contexts is intricately rooted in people's worldviews. They don't recognize that they have original sin. It is a difficult idea for them to process. Explanation of nature and force of original sin through the exposition of Romans 7:18–21 may be of help:

> For I know that good itself does not dwell in me, that is, in my sinful nature. For I have the desire to do what is good, but I cannot carry it out. For I do not do the good I want to do, but the evil I do not want to do—this I keep on doing. Now if I do what I do not want to do, it is no longer I who do it, but it is sin living in me that does it. So I find this law at work: Although I want to do good, evil is right there with me.

The fall of mankind through Adam and Eve is also to be indicated to expound on the root of original sin. Otherwise, your Buddhist neighbor may not see the need to recognize the sin, which leads to no need for forgiveness, which then leads to no need for the

Savior. In Buddhism, sin is perceived as ignorance and isn't eventually immoral. It is understood as a misstep rather than a transgression against God's holiness. The nature of sin and its consequences ought to be explained to Buddhist friends to help them see the point of forgiveness and salvation through Jesus Christ. Otherwise, the concept of salvation may just remain foreign to them.

Since Buddhism believes in life after death, this commonality can trigger a discussion about the afterlife. Ephesians 2:8 will serve as an important reminder to them because of the influence of the Eightfold Paths[33] on their initial worldview, taking their earned merits to reach a state of *nirvana* (liberation from an endless cycle of rebirths).

> For it is by grace you have been saved, through faith—and this is not from yourselves, it is the gift of God . . . (Ephesians 2:8)

Lastly, the Buddhist's pluralistic religious view that all religions are good challenges the uniqueness of Christ and the gospel. People may even accept the gospel message swiftly but classify Jesus as a religious leader or a god among others. Missionaries should share with Buddhists about the indefinite and unique nature of God the Creator and his relationship with his creations. Buddhism pursues buddha-hood by following Eightfold Paths, including meditation, to achieve emptiness and good works to go beyond *karma* (consequences) of life. The goal is to gain enlightenment and rebirth.[34] In contrast, Christ wants his followers to fill themselves with his presence. Only then, the right heart, right thinking, and right actions will be brought forth out of human nature that was once corrupt by sin. Presentation of Christ's identity and emphasis of his divinity is a powerful element one should not forget in his witnessing effort to Buddhists. Gautama Buddha never claimed to be divine, but rather a man who shows the way of life to others. Yet, Jesus' apparent proclamation of his divine identity is striking. Jesus

---

33. Namely (1) right understanding, (2) right thought, (3) right speech, (4) right action, (5) right livelihood, (6) right effort, (7) right mindfulness, and (8) right concentration.

34. For detail articulation of Eightfold Paths of Buddhism, see Bodhi, *The Noble Eightfold Path*.

claimed to be God's Son (Matthew 3:17). Jesus and God are one (John 10:30). There are many other Bible verses that portray Jesus' divinity, including John 1:1; 1:14; 1:18; 5:18; 10:33; 14:6; 17:21; Colossians 2:9–10; Philippians 2:5–6; and 1 John 5:20. Sharing such Scriptures can be a stimulating thought to your Buddhist neighbor as the Holy Spirit triggers his curiosity on Jesus' identity and deity.

While keeping solemn respect for the Buddhists and their religion, it is recommended to use the indirect self-discovery method to guide them to the genuine truth. It'll be wise to avoid direct comparison between Jesus and Buddha. Indirect and gentle guidance along with patience is key. Inductive discovery of contrasting differences between Jesus and Buddha can create a crack in their souls.

In Denominational Protectionism Society

One more society that shouldn't be ignored for Christian persecution is a denominational protectionism society. It may not be easy for some people to grasp why so-called Christians persecute other brothers. Sadly, it has been a reality in history. For one, Eritrean Christians from non-traditional denominations face one of the harshest persecutions from the totalitarian government and the Eritrean Orthodox Church (EOC) as well. EOC is the only Christian denomination recognized by the government in the nation. Non-EOC members including, but not limited to, MBCs suffer dire harassment from family, neighbors, and the local authority. Their social rights are often overlooked and undermined under the tight control of the powerful. Even in some parts of China, it has been orally reported that the Three-Self Patriotic Church, the government-recognized Christian denomination, is occasionally in cooperation with the communist government to oppress unregistered house churches and other underground churches.

It is quite unfortunate that the fierce persecution of non-EOC members in Eritrea as well as Ethiopia is underreported in the body of Christ simply because they were inflicted on them by their fellow brothers against everyone's expectation. Tibebe Eshete, an Ethiopian professor, once wrote about how Evangelicals, especially Pentecostals, had to endure multiple persecutions in this setting.

The growth of Pentecostals with emphasis on the individual experience of conversion was deemed a threat to the control and unity of Ethiopia as a nation and the Ethiopian Orthodox Church as a denomination. The 1970s was vividly marked as a dark tunnel period for this newly initiated movement. Neither the government and Orthodox Church were ready for the unconventional and exponential expansion of evangelical churches and therefore put a brake on their rapid propagation. This led to the persecution of two different types all at the same time. The fire-tested Pentecostals faced even harder persecution from an atheistic Marxist regime after the 1974 revolution, but they were ready for it. They eventually saw paradoxical additional growth.

Persecution from denominational protectionism is heavily flawed as to render the unbiblical abuse of power and serious failure to be a brother's keeper. God's idea of bestowing power on Christians is for godly impact on others. Christians ought to be after influence, not enforcement, on society. Any Christian usage of power for his personal gain is short of the biblical design of God-given authority. The signet ring of every hero of faith and influence recorded in the Bible was flawlessly inscribed in this pericope: "*The Lord was with him.*(Genesis 21:22; 26:28; 39:2–3; 39:21; 39:23; Joshua 6:27; Judges 6:12; 1 Samuel 16:18; 17:3; 18:12; 18:14; 18:28; 2 Samuel 5:10; 7:3; 2 Kings 18:7; 2 Chronicles 1:1; 15:9; Luke 1:28).

Godly influence flowing through the man and woman who have been with the Lord touched countless lives and communities in history. David's early life was marked with that notable condition. Nevertheless, it is noteworthy that we do not see the same statement anywhere in the Bible while he was committing adultery with Bathsheba. It is well motioned in Nathan's parable, which wisely led to his rebuke of David. The rich man abused his power to take the one and only lamb of the poor man. Likewise, it was the first time the Bible records that the man after God's own heart used his power to bring a married woman to his chamber for the fulfillment of his pleasure and gain. God wasn't pleased with David's action and the fear of the Lord left David in that segment of his life.

Void of the awareness of God's presence and compassion, denominational protectionism severely tampers with the biblical exercise of spiritual authority over others. History is full of such misuses of authority and mistreatment of subjects, from blood-marked crusades in the Middle East to Charlemagne's "divine right to rule" over Europe. God gave the authority and power to certain individuals in his church so that they might serve other fellow human beings, not lord it over those entrusted to them but be examples to others as 1 Peter 5:3 instructs. Besides, the biblical authority requires responsibility taken in action. An abusive husband who takes no responsibility for his wife equally has no authority over her. A guest speaker who has no responsibility for the local church has no ongoing authority in the church. Christians who do not love the community and care for its needs will not likely be able to take authority over the community in the name of Christ.[35]

LOVE THY NEIGHBOR

Once converted, helping new believers and nurturing them in spiritual and relational haven is vitally important, even more so for those who follow Christ in anti-Christian religious society due to the nature of pressuring environment. A nest of discipleship should be provided in the form of a vibrant small group where they can be guided. This is a critical assignment and can't be overemphasized.

Many converts from Islam have either little or no connection with one another.[36] Twenty scholars came together to discuss and compile a combined volume of researches done on the issues related to MBCs. David Greenlee points out in the subsequential volume, *Longing for Community*, that we often fail to invest time and energy in preparing Christians to receive the MBCs into the community. Out of their zeal to win new souls, missionaries and mission strategists sometimes overlook discipling souls that are already won. The MBCs dearly long for a Christian version of *ummah* (the Islamic concept of community where both spiritual and physical needs are met for the Muslims) in the body of Christ.[37] As is in the case of many new converts, when an MBC chooses to follow Christ, he

---

35. Norman, *A Tree of Life*, 139.
36. Jørgensen, *Jesus Imandars and Christ Bhaktas*, 34.
37. Greenlee, *Longing for Community*, 78.

may fail to fully process how he was drawn to the Lord and to grow into discipleship on a basis of the biblical worldview. Unfortunately, a large number of MBCs are left hanging, unaccepted and unwelcomed by both the Muslim community who consider them apostates and the Christian community who doubt the genuineness of their conversion.[38]

This is one task every missionary to Muslims must be mindful of in their ministry strategy. The value of finding a Christian community and being a part of it stands the test of time and place. If one can't find for himself a community nearby, he might as well need to create one lest he tumbles off a course with no one to help. While some do criticize the need for the insider movement, guiding the converts from a Muslim background to realign their identity in Christ in a transitional process should not be ignored, whether they stay in disguise as Muslims or seek to abide in a more "Christian" form of community.[39]

Christians should stop acting as if the devout of other religions are enemies of Christ. They're not our enemies, but the devil—the deceiver—is. The more Christians propagate anti-pagan messages (instead of the pure message of the gospel), the harder missionary incarnation takes place in their outreach efforts. Hard to grasp but undeniably true, our persecutors also deserve the gospel and God's mercy. As it was told long ago, you will never look into the eyes of someone God does not love.

Last but not least, regarding financial contribution to help persecuted believers in anti-Christian religious societies, we still need to exercise shrewd observation and normative stewardship. Sad cases of donation seekers of ill motives have been reported in the past among those who advocate for the persecuted. Seeking financial support out of good-willed Western donors, exaggerated numbers of converts from Islam were occasionally given out. We shouldn't forget that it's difficult to verify their numbers because most of them act in secrecy. There were reports of Bangladeshis being hired as showcase converts to solicit extra donations from

---

38. Greenlee, *Longing for Community*, 71.
39. Farrokh, "Perceptions of Muslim Identity," 247–48.

visiting supporters. Visitors soon discovered that they were generally ignorant of Christianity in their conversations with them.[40]

Some of the creative ideas and practical suggestions that were field-tested on the CAR fields with anti-Christian predilection have been introduced and suggested in this chapter. You'll still need to draw out tactile understanding and real-world wisdom that are applicable in your own setting, as Proverbs 20:5 affirms: "Though good advice lies deep within the heart, a person with understanding will draw it out" (NLT). May the Lord give you wisdom and the Holy Spirit guide you as you do so.

---

40. Croft, "Muslim Background Believers in Bangladesh," 10.

5

Mission in Atheistic Society

ATHEIST IDENTITY

Atheism can be found from the individualistic mindset in the West to statewide ideology in the East. Atheism is a belief that God does not exist. The community of American atheists is mostly upheld on an individual basis, widely scattered and steadily fostered through the media. American atheism has its communal roots in the deism and freethought movements of previous centuries. It was in the twentieth century when several incongruent anti-religious groups found their way into organizing a stream of atheistic camps. Well-known figures like Charles Lee Smith and Madalyn Murray O'Hair led the way. The New Atheism movement found its way into the stream in 2004, and prolific authors like Richard Dawkins, Sam Harris, and the late Christopher Hitchens were up front, questioning the validity of the faiths of Christianity and Islam for a lack of empirical evidence. Mostly through media and mass gatherings for Americans dissatisfied with predominant religious culture, atheism has developed social structure and public identification that is no longer insignificant and that can't be now overlooked at the beginning of the twenty-first century.[1]

---

1. Chalfant, "Atheism in America."

I personally tend to perceive that an atheist is a person who takes a notion of running away from God or at least denying his involvement. Otherwise, they would have not coined themselves as a-theists, still indicating the name of God on their label instead of calling themselves with a term that is entirely void of God's name. Most of them have had some sort of negative experience with or influence from religion in the past—not necessarily God himself—which conceivably triggered them to poise their stand toward becoming an atheist.

Jesse Smith's research reveals four major elements in the construction of an atheist identity in America: (1) the starting point—the ubiquity of theism, (2) questioning theism, (3) rejecting theism, and (4) "coming out" atheist. These elements are described in a general sense for the stages involved in one's progression toward atheism for the sake of simplicity, yet the real process involves more fluid and complex issues. It isn't standardized.[2] As you can see from the first element "the ubiquity of theism," it is no wonder that some atheists come from a religious background. It owes most likely to the lack of pertinent mentors around him by the time the person reaches the second stage of "questioning theism."

Being an atheist has earned a community identity in the West through much of its social networking.[3] More and more are finding themselves believing vigorously that human society is better off without religion because they think religion is useless or even poisonous. Often, the impact of atheism on society tends to be more expressive and graver than atheism itself as a governing philosophy. While the United States has stayed, by and large, with its religious flavor for past centuries, post-Christian America is undoubtedly on the horizon. Ross Douthat's alarming article in *The New York Times*, "Waking Up in 2030,"[4] predicts that the recession of religion will be expedited in the post-COVID world, causing both Protestants and Catholics to experience an eventual decline in giving and attendance. Indisputably, the influence of faith on our lives and our ability to communicate the meaning of the Christian tradition with

---

2. Smith, "Becoming an Atheist in America," 219.
3. Smith, "Creating a Godless Community," 80–99.
4. Douthat, "Waking Up in 2030."

the world hasn't been the same. Sad to admit, an atheistic America is around the corner. Failure to take the contemporary societal changes into account for re-evaluation through effective Christian witness in the current generation will cause a serious blow on the prophetic role and longevity of the church in coming generations.[5]

ATHEISTIC NATIONS

In many parts of the world outside of the United States, atheism has somewhat become another form of religion in itself, the very thing it despises and hates.[6] It isn't difficult to notice that atheism was the state "religion" of the former Soviet Union, in much the same way as Christianity became the state religion of the Roman Empire under the influence of Constantine.[7]

There are nations, communities, and societies that are far more systematically governed by an atheistic mindset in this world. Communist countries are but one of them. Although we saw a drastic demise of Marxism and communism after the fall of the Soviet Union, the world has yet to witness the demise of their atheistic roots governing the remaining communist states and other nations influenced by the ideology. In such contexts, one's gospel presentation must begin with a point that God does exist, unlike anti-Christian religious societies.

Our work in China and Vietnam had to first understand this atheistic culture by which people were saturated, though they are now heavily obsessed with materialism in the place of God. In gospel-restricted cultures, including atheistic nations, foreign organizations may face opposition and hostility to settling on local soil, while indigenous organizations that are formed or led by locals can get easier acceptance. Partnering with like-minded local organizations is one strategy a missionary can consider adapting toward mission effectiveness.

---

5. Noble, *Disruptive Witness*, 175.
6. See Hedges, *When Atheism Becomes Religion*.
7. McGrath, *The Twilight of Atheism*, 168.

POWER OF BUSINESS AND EDUCATION

Effective strategies usually include indirect approaches through the means of *business* and *education*. Both are largely welcomed in atheistic nations. The outward disguise of such labels may provide security for inward gospel sharing. It can also assist in issuing a stay-visa for a missionary and his family with a long-term commitment to the field work. Besides, forming corporate entrepreneurship can have a great impact on local employees, who often unconsciously accept and identify with the culture of the company they work for. If a business is run with Christian principles at the core of its particular corporate culture, it is natural for employees to indirectly get to know the Christian faith, regardless of their cultural or religious prejudice. Business-as-mission (BAM) has its merit in gospel-restricted countries, including atheistic states.

Education is another strategic approach. School is one of the best places to break in. Even if it is not allowed to share the gospel directly to students because of local policies, the idea of education centered on the Christian principle might as well contribute to the healthy growth and moral development of students. This societal feature can be regarded as a precursor to the gospel ministry. In addition to basic education, other types of vocational educations or training institutions can be considered as another preparatory step to gospel sharing. The first step in evangelism is to establish a relationship with people and to develop in them an indirect interest in Christ.

In Vietnam, it shows that one of the strategic approaches to cultural change is education. Choosing the right education for excellence is in great demand in many growing, industrial, and competitive communist countries like Vietnam and China. Christian missions have cracks to penetrate those nations through open doors in the education sector. It can cause a change in the future of one family, one community, and one nation at a time.

Dealing with problems of cultural misleading and outdated customs remains challenging for organizations—and even a government. We need a transformative education and outreach plan with a specific roadmap and strategy to change the worldview and culture of a target group. Even so, the Holy Spirit moves in all cultures, as he uses his servants to transform the target group with the light of the gospel. Missionaries must be sensitive to the move of the Holy Spirit and obey his lead for the fruitful ministry of culture transformation.

Additionally, marginalized sectors of children and women in societies almost always welcome salvific hands from missionaries. Those doors can also lead them to connect with the nitty-gritty needs of the local community and open their hearts to the gospel message. Eunice has found herself at home in many corners of the world and served in missions alongside me with her expertise in children's ministry. Involved in the children's ministry from 1984 as a Sunday school teacher, she's touched countless souls of children both in the US and overseas. A wide spectrum of her children's ministry, including children's gospel campaigns, vacation Bible schools, and Bible camps, has helped scores of missionaries in Uzbekistan, South America, East Africa, Korea, and Asia at large.

She regularly reminds Christians about the importance of children's ministry. She often asserted that children are the greatest mission field. A study shows that 85 percent of people come to Christ before the age of eighteen. By the time a child is nine years old, his/her basic moral foundation has been formed. By the age of thirteen, a child has formed their basic beliefs about the nature of God, the reliability of the Bible, the existence of an afterlife, and Christ's sacrificial love.[8] Thus, this is a ministry at the most critical time of a person's life. The early years are the most formative period. Above and beyond, children are everywhere in any part of the world. About 26 percent of the world is under fifteen years of age.[9] First Timothy 2:4 affirms that God desires *all people* to be saved and to come to the knowledge of the truth. We must remember that children are well included in *all people*. Also, children's ministry was a priority for Jesus. The disciples didn't think it should be, but Jesus did. He made time to minister to children. He commanded the disciples to let the little children come to him and not to hinder them (Matthew 19:14; Mark 10:14). Jesus loves and

---

8. Barna Group, "Evangelism Is Most Effective among Kids"; Brewster, "The 4/14 Window."

9. Szmigiera, "World Population by Age and Region 2021."

values children. Children's ministry can be a highly effective strategy for church growth as well. It's common sense that when you reach children you have earned free access to their families.[10]

SOFT SPOT FOR CHILDREN'S MINISTRY

After all, children are not just the church of tomorrow. They are the church of today. We need to raise the leaders of their generation. Children who understand God's love and how to love their neighbors will impact their generation for Christ. Eunice recalls a child named Shany, a six-year-old girl from the socialist country of Tanzania, East Africa. Her family was Muslim. She came to the kindergarten which Eunice was directing in Nairobi, Kenya—a neighboring country of Tanzania. After attending the school for a while, her love for the Bible story grew. One day, she decided to have Jesus as her Lord and friend. Her mother also became a Christian through Shany's influence. Later when she was about to return to Tanzania, she asked Eunice and other teachers to pray for her to keep her faith and to be a missionary to her people.

The story of Cletus and Monica Tukai is another prevailing anecdote of what God can do in a hard-soiled community through educational ministry for children. Tanzania was under the rule of a socialist government. Every housewasis under the surveillance of a warden. It wasn't easy to penetrate the Moshi community when the Tukais arrived as missionaries dispatched by EAPTC Kenya. They testified that it was like hitting a rock with an egg for the first few years. This missionary couple began to look after the needs of their neighbors and participated in community events (with an exception of ungodly rituals and practices). Following their passion, they took deserted children of the community—one by one—and raised them as if they were their own children. Their reputation of being good Samaritans gradually grew. One of the greatest needs of the community was AIDS victims, especially the abandoned children of parents with AIDS. Sometimes babies were deserted at a dumping ground. When they heard about Tukais, the HIV-infected parents who couldn't afford to raise their baby left him/her at their doorstep in

10. Phelps, "How Valuable Is Children's Ministry?"

the night. Cletus and Monica took them as their own and took care of them. Soon, the local police noticed their merits and provided legal protection to set up an orphanage as the number of children increased. Their sacrificial love for children melted the heart of the stone-like community in the socialist country.

The children's ministry of Cletus and Monica ran in two folds: (1) to look after orphans, and (2) to educate children of all backgrounds by establishing a primary school. Also, English-language education was becoming a booming trend in Kiswahili-speaking Tanzania. Natives of Kenya, where both English and Kiswahili are used as the languages of instruction in all secondary schools, the Tukais were fluent in English and seized this opportunity. They opened an English class and utilized it as a means to introduce people to Bible verses and Christian faith. Over the years, their children's ministry and educational ministry built a bridge with the cold-hearted community they went to reach. After a decade of selfless ministry, Christ's aroma kept spreading in the Moshi community. Today, the work continues in other parts of Tanzania and neighboring Kiswahili-speaking countries through their disciples, who caught their vision and replicated their work.

These are only a few of countless stories of how children's ministry helped transform community and culture in atheistic nations. Children's ministry is more than teaching Bible knowledge or Christian customs. It is about touching the hearts of children with God's word and Jesus' love through teachers' Christ-centered lifestyle. I witnessed many parents testifying how Eunice and her children's ministry teams served as good examples of Christ's love. It ultimately created in them ripple effects of gospel sharing to their extended families and relatives. Their school ministry to children has sown the seeds of the gospel and opened many doors for my ministry in Africa and Asia, especially in gospel-restricted communities.

Once people in atheistic societies see the goodness of Christ and his life-changing power, their eyes can be opened. They'll get interested in the gospel from an individual level. With a substantial amount of good reputation and ripple effect of individuals added to reach the level of community impact, the change will come in God's due time.

6

Mission in Metamodern Society

AMERICA, A SINKING SHIP?

The culture in America and the world at large is tectonically changing. Pew Research shows that American teens are less likely to identify themselves as Christian than their parents' generation. The new study found that only 63 percent of US teenagers aged between thirteen and seventeen identify as Christian, while their parents responded with a 72-percent mark. On the other end, American teens are more likely than their parents to identify as religious "nones" (32 percent versus 24 percent).[1] The term "nones" refers to those who claim to be either atheist, agnostic or non-religious whatsoever.

In the United States, 62 percent of unchurched folks reported to have attended church in the past but stopped. Reasons vary but are categorized mainly as (1) having lost trust in the church, (2) losing interest in the church, and (3) circumstances changed to lead toward unchurched life.[2] As we see increasing numbers of the unchurched population, whether or not they claim to be Christians, the need for more Christian mentors (not just by talks but by walks) is immense for millennials and the next generations.

---

1. Pew Research Center, "1. Religious Affiliation among American Adolescents."
2. Richardson, *You Found Me*, 45–48.

I don't believe American Christianity is a sinking ship. Nor is European Christianity. Indeed, a shift of Christian demography from the Global North to the Global South has already taken place. However, my missionary experience of serving on three continents tells me that God always reserves *seven thousand* faithfuls everywhere whose knees have not bowed down to Baal and whose mouths have not kissed him (1 Kings 19:18). God still has a plan for the churches and mission agencies in North America (and Europe) to continue to excel in world mission. Yet, only adequately Scripture-exegeted churches and missions will pull through in the millennial generation—not with a misinterpreted view of mission that is polluted with a colonial mindset, as it was once in the dark past. Scripture needs to be taught, meditated, and applied thoroughly in our churches and other Christian teaching ministries with respect to the changing religious landscape.

The next generation is a post-postmodern generation, or is referred to as the "metamodern generation." Sunday service attendance is becoming a fringe activity more and more (even for Christians), and church members are increasingly found unaware of exactly what they believe as Christians.[3] This chapter is dedicated to elaborating on this challenging culture of post-postmodernism or metamodernism to turn it around to be a carrier of the gospel and missions.

WHAT IS METAMODERNISM?

Metamodernism stemmed from the latest notion of postmodernism, which traces its root in its predecessor—modernism. The late modernism had a raging impact on the faith community in the United States and around the world. The global influence of modernism delineated the grouping of American Protestant churches into modernists, Evangelicals, and fundamentalists (who were later merged into the Evangelicals' group). In Protestantism, those who believed the Bible is beneficial but needed to be rewritten to suit modern thinkings were considered modernists. Others who believed

---

3. Nieuwhof, "10 Things that Demonstrate the World You Grew Up in No Longer Exists."

in the inerrancy of the Bible and segregated themselves from those who upheld evolutionary theory and possible Biblical errancy were categorized as fundamentalists. One who believed in the inerrancy of the Bible but was tolerable to the contemporary culture, science, and thoughts to cooperate with people who didn't share all their beliefs were labeled "neo-Evangelicals" or simply "Evangelicals."[4] The modern era (1750–1900) mainly took the source of authority from reason. The postmodern era (1900–2010) took it from personal experiences.[5] The ethos of postmodernism rejected the notion that there's an authoritative and unified voice, which accounts for the whole of life.[6] Recently, the classic postmodernism was subsequently morphed into the next form of its philosophical perspective—namely post-postmodernism or metamodernism. The generations that learn things more from the internet and YouTube than from teachers in face to face meetings have sprung up everywhere, from secularized Europe to once-conservative Islamic nations. Cross-cultural and cross-generational understanding of metamodern society will be of absolute necessity as we launch Christ's mission to make disciples of all nations (and all generations). The below table narrates a comparison of modernism, postmodernism, and post-postmodernism at a glance.[7]

---

4. Lea, "Phil Vischer: What Is an Evangelical, Really?"
5. See Webber, *Ancient-future Faith*.
6. See Lyotard, *The Postmodern Condition*.
7. Cooper, "'Beyond' Metamodernism." Used with permission.

	MODERN thesis	POST-MODERN antithesis	POST-POSTMODERN synthesis
	declarative	reactive	integrative synthetic (logic)
VIEW	absolutism	relative	perspectival (frames of reference)
	grand narrative	subjectivity	meta-narrative
KNOWLEDGE	empiricism	hermeneutic discourse	transdisciplinary injunctions (integral methodological pluralism)
	discoverable	inventible (constructed)	actionable – enactment
MEANING	content	context	context independent (grades / hierarchies)
APTITUDES	senses	mediated discourse	meta-theory
EXPLAIN	perception	language	patterns
PROCESS	mechanical	relational	developmental
DOMAIN	nature	culture	global/planetary
ETHICS	"Good"	relativistic situational	authentic
MAKE	abstraction	deconstruction	meta-construction
MORALITY	principle	"Right"	spirituality

Adapted with permission from a video presentation by Bonnitta Roy: From Postmodernism to Post-PoMo (2012) (part 1 of the Magellan Course series)
Reddit.com/r/PostPoMo – facebook.com/PostPoMo

Table 2. Comparison of Modernism, Postmodernism, and Metamodernism

In 1973, economist Georges Anderla created a statistical study of years taken to double the sum of human knowledge while working with the Organization for Economic Cooperation and Development (OECD). Here is what he found out.[8]

- First doubling took AD 1 to 1500.
- Second doubling, 1500 to 1750.
- Third doubling, 1750 to 1900.
- Fourth doubling, 1900 and 1950.

8. Dey et al., "Knowledge Abstraction Levels."

- Fifth doubling, 1950 to 1960.
- Sixth doubling, 1960 to 1967.
- Seventh doubling, 1967 to 1972.

Knowledge is increasing and is doing so more rapidly as the days of the Lord's return get nearer.

> Many shall run to and fro, and knowledge shall be increased. (Daniel 12:4b, KJV)

Unlike previous generations, it became readily available to learn anything (whether it is true or false) on the internet. Internet usage from a cell phone has reached 55.1 percent of the world population by January 2021.[9] With this smartphone-savvy generation, the traditional role of teachers may need to be altered to adapt to contemporary changes. Online education has expedited to a full gallop and became an essential part of the teaching mechanism along with in-person class meetings.

Yet, a suitcase attached to the said advancement consequentially follows. A poll conducted in 2014 revealed that the average time students cut out from watching their teaching videos on online education was less than six minutes.[10] Another research prior to this poll showed that it averaged ten minutes,[11] which tells us that people progressively lose their interest in online content unless it's attractive and "stylish." We now tend to even modify worship. I once heard a pastor rebuking his church members for the rampant practice of fast-forwarding, increasing playback speed, and skipping content while listening to a sermon at an online worship service. In fact, it has become a common phenomenon. After online education was widely adopted by many learning institutions as a part of the new normal during the COVID-19 pandemic, increasing numbers of cheating activities were reported at the private Christian school where I serve on the board of trustees. I have a hunch that the frequency may be higher in public schools.

---

9. Johnson, "Worldwide Digital Population as of January 2021."
10. Guo et al., "How Video Production Affects Student Engagement."
11. Medina, *Brain Rules*, 74, 89–93.

Teachers' authority may as well be challenged to a greater scope. In this scenario, teachers will no longer be "the sage on the stage." Often, a Google search may provide more vast and updated information than human teachers who might have missed the latest news in any academic discipline. Therefore, mentors, not necessarily teachers, will be in greater demand for postmodernists and metamodernists. Mentors should be willing to serve as coaches and guides, not just information transmitters.[12] In this sense, teachers in metamodern society are prone to develop more interpersonal skills and leadership traits by mentoring others. They can also find greater potential to grow as teachers than those of previous generations.[13] Teaching in the postmodern or metamodern society requires a meta-curriculum "which is concerned with the creative and critical activity of mapmaking rather than with the content of any specific map."[14] Also, a teaching model of leading students to critical thinking and rational autonomy rather than memorization and indoctrination will be far more penetrative for teachers of the metamodern generation.[15] This is why interdisciplinary studies can pave the way to create better chances to connect with the metamodern society.

Metamodern theorist Hanzi Freinacht defines metamodernism as a synthesis of modernism and postmodernism. Metamodernism is a philosophical perspective which combines extreme irony with unyielding sincerity, he claims in the book *The Listening Society*.[16] As early as the nineteenth century, when the world began to deem that Christianity was emptied of all its meaning and content, the concept has moved beyond the absence of God. While a notion of "the death of God" was popularized by Nietzsche and Hegel, among others, "a kind of felicitous nominalism, a happy, anti-essentialist open-endedness" was recognized and promoted in this notion.[17]

---

12. Eby et al., "Definition and Evolution of Mentoring," 7–20.
13. Rekha and Ganesh, "Do Mentors Learn by Mentoring Others?"
14. Lester, "Learning for the 21st Century," 9.
15. Reichard, "From Indoctrination to Initiation," 285–99.
16. See Freinacht, *The Listening Society*.
17. Caputo, *More Radical Hermeneutics*, 16.

At the same time, the body of Christ was seen no longer credible by people in society.[18] Nominalism of religion was engraved in the hearts of people, even to the point of theological liberalism being introduced.[19] All these escalated to the arrival of postmodernism, a forerunner of metamodernism. The term "metamodernism" was coined in 2010 by Timotheus Vermeulen and Robin van den Akker to identify post-postmodern thought which attempted to reconcile aspects of both modernism and postmodernism.[20] The time has arrived for the body of Christ to seriously consider doing missions with strategies which promote low cost and high efficiency and are relevant to contemporary contexts rather than clinging to high-cost and low-efficiency and irrelevant to the changing culture. We must go beyond a mission strategy operating merely with the status quo. It is high time now to seek excellence in missions.

DISADVANTAGE AGAINST CHRISTIAN MISSION

Evangelical churches typically list three principles of authority: (1) experience, (2) the Scriptures, and (3) reason.[21] In the Bible, we find various types of authority delegated to human society: the authority of Christ (Ephesians 1:22), the authority of human leaders whom God appointed (Hebrews 13:17), the governing authority (Romans 13:1), the customary authority (1 Corinthians 11:2–16), and the authority of conscience (Romans 2:14–15).

With its tenets born in modernist concepts, postmodernism has heavily dismantled the biblical elements of authority. A devious metamodern worldview, just like postmodernism, assimilates no authority and no absolute truth and thus hampers acceptance of the gospel truth. Both postmodernism and metamodernism stand antithetical to the Christian mission that propagates the monotheistic worldview by proclaiming that Christ is the way and the truth and the life (John 14:6).

---

18. McGrath and Marks, *The Blackwell Companion to Protestantism*, 454.
19. McGrath and Marks, *The Blackwell Companion to Protestantism*, 458.
20. Vermeulen and Akker, "Notes on Metamodernism," 5677.
21. Beckwith, "The Types of Authority in Christian Belief," 241–52.

Many Hollywood movies vividly reflect those metamodern distinctive. Good and bad are not crystal clear anymore. Sometimes, thieves and murderers are depicted as attractive, advanced, and even "cool" characters. Both heroes and villains are portrayed as vulnerable, open-ended figures who are good and not good at the same time. Either end is acceptable and reconcilable. They leave judgment of good and evil to individuals, while the Bible reminds us that it is God and his word which draws the line between the two. Trying to distinguish good and evil outside the principles of God and his word eventually results in our spiritual deaths.

> But you must not eat from the tree of the knowledge of good and evil, for when you eat from it you will certainly die. (Genesis 2:17)

When everyone did as they saw fit in the time of Judges, it led people only into chaos and delusion (Judges 21:25). Metamodernists advocate a similar notion and refuse to acknowledge the authority that they have not validated firsthand. The book *Correcting the Cults* points out the growth of relativism in our culture. The concepts of secular humanism are rampantly expressed today in day-to-day expressions like "That may be true for you but not for me," "Do your own thing," and "Everything is relative to the situation." Because society has denied God-given absolutes of Judeo-Christian value, it has been sadly left with a God-sized vacuum in human souls.[22]

A teacher can have only minimal authority over students by title, but for him to have an influence over them it takes an earned authority. Although it is universally applicable to everyone in a sense, earning authority and respect through relationship building will be of greater necessity to influence and lead metamodernists. Such authority is gained through assuming responsibility with accountability, even more so in metamodern society.

---

22. Geisler and Rhodes, *Correcting the Cults*, 15.

ADVANTAGE FOR CHRISTIAN MISSION

Although postmodernism and metamodernism stand antithetical to the Christian mission in their dichotomy, some of their characteristics may be used for the benefit of the Christian mission. The main feature of such characteristics is their open-endedness. About this intriguing idea, Mary Koutselini put it this way.

> [Metamodernism] transcends the deterministic closed system of physical reality and supports change, interaction, and transaction . . . it also implies a shift in how we think about the human relationship to the world, a shift that leads us beyond the sequential, quantifiable understanding of the universe and promotes the experience of a network of relationships, with the individual having the central voice. Consequently, experience and reflections on the experience emphasize qualitative processes instead of quantitative results.[23]

Concisely put, metamodernism defines person by actions, not by descriptions.[24] Here is the advantage point. Valuing personal experiences can be used as a favorable tool for the Christian mission to win postmodernists and metamodernists for Christ. It can be a powerful mechanism of communication to penetrate metamodern society. Narrative testimonials of one's encounter with Christ, combined with tireless personal cares, get to encourage and to connect them to the introduction of Jesus in their own pace and ways.

After all, God is deemed dead to postmodernists most likely because they haven't seen enough Christlike Christians around. It wasn't the death of God but rather their experience of shortage in an encounter with genuine Christians. Worldview is a powerful gear-shifting instrument that forms cultures and runs human behaviors. Just like postmodernism, the devious worldview of this metamodernism assimilates no authority and no absolute truth, which directly challenges the proclamation of the gospel truth. Yet, since metamodernism values personal experiences, the narrative of one's testimony can be an effective tool to reach metamodernists.

---

23. Koutselini, "Towards a Meta-modern Paradigm of Curriculum," 4.
24. See Gladwell, *Blink*, 31.

Moreover, follow-ups with genuine love and care can serve as ways to lead them to the ultimate *veritas*—Christ. As John Montgomery once stated, if an average person put as much time into investigating Christianity as he put into a college humanities course, most of these people would come to faith.[25] Unless one is slothful in searching for truth, there is a fair chance for the person to find *veritas* as we pray for him with a supporting attitude. Yet someone needs to be there for him to see what Christ is like in the process of his search. That is where we can be deliberately used by God to lead metamodernists closer to Christ.

WEARING CHRIST'S COAT

> Beloved, I beg you as sojourners and pilgrims, abstain from fleshly lusts which war against the soul, having your conduct honorable among the gentiles, that when they speak against you as evildoers, they may, *by your good works which they observe*, glorify God in the day of visitation. (1 Peter 2:11–12, NKJV, emphasis added)

A rumor has it that Mahatma Gandhi once confessed, "If it weren't for Christians, I'd be a Christian."[26] While it is debatable whether or not Gandhi actually said that, the particular statement contains a valuable message for Christians to take heed if we're serious about reaching people in the metamodern society. Churches that fail to incarnate into society especially by looking after the needs of the poor and the community at large will massively fail to connect with the metamodern world.

Bosch termed the practice of incarnation theology as Christians who agonize, sweat, and bleed together with the poor and oppressed. Some churches have an idealist understanding of their identity but fail to practice offering a home for masters as well as slaves, rich and poor, oppressor and oppressed. Churches that undermine the needs of victims in society cease to have relevance to

---

25. Groothuis, *Christian Apologetics*, 155.
26. Carson, "If It Weren't for Christians, I'd Be a Christian—Gandhi."

the hurting world. Losing such a social dimension of the gospel message, churches have corrupted their original nature.[27]

In the book *Of Whom the World Was Not Worthy*, Marie Chapian speaks of another abusive ecclesiastical system in cooperation with the powerful of the land in former Yugoslavia that paralyzed a true church. It was another form of denominational protectionism exploiting others in the name of God. Acutely corrupted, church officials threatened the livelihood of innocent people and devoured their land at will.

A Christian evangelist named Jakob visits a village and comforts Cimmerman, an old man who found Christianity dreadful for what the church had done to his villagers by looting and exploiting them. Jakov, looking for an occasion to get Cimmerman to change his line of thinking, uses an analogy of a coat and asks him:

> Cimmerman, can I ask you a question? Suppose I were to steal your coat, put it on, and break into a bank. Suppose further that the police sighted me running in the distance but could not catch up with me. One clue, however, put them onto your track; they recognized your coat. What would you say to them if they came to your house and accused you of breaking into the bank?

Cimmerman was quick-witted and annoyed at where the conversation was going. Jakov left but returned regularly and shared Christ's love with Cimmerman over the years. Overwhelmed by Jakov's genuine love, one day Cimmerman invited Christ into his life. On the day of his conversion, Cimmerman pointed the heaven and told Jakov, "You wear his coat very well."[28]

In the metamodern culture, the name of Christ is mostly misrepresented by so-called Christians who wore Christ's coat wrongly and weren't patient enough to reflect him to others. Christian preaching or literature is of a minimal impact unless it is lived out by somebody. In this regard, the church has made a series of mistakes throughout history. Yes, the church needs to feel sorry for hurting the people. Yet the people also need to know it was humanity, not Jesus or the teachings of the Bible. Too often, ill-presented

---

27. Bosch, *Transforming Mission*, 525.
28. Chapian, *Of Whom the World Was Not Worthy*, 122–23.

and misrepresented Christianity has done more damages to mission and evangelism efforts than Christianity that kept silent over injustice and suffering of society while both are certainly not what Christ had in mind for his body on earth. Many postmodernists and metamodernists have been turned off by organized religion and religious institutions.[29] The church was, and is, a movement, not organized religion or religious institution, from her very inception, as attested throughout the book of Acts.

Merely focusing on the ill-traits of different beliefs and perspectives metamodernists subscribe to rather than on their strengths and beauties can be an unwise approach that widens the chasm between the church and society. Respectfully not belittling the differing opinions but trusting the power of Christ to change lives and treating everyone equally with love will pay off in due time. A survey shows that Gen Z generally doesn't consider the church as a safe place for them to open up for conversations and, if necessary, express doubt. Furthermore, the generation is starving for someone who will listen without judgment, demonstrate confidence in sharing their own perspective, show interest in other people's story or life, is good at asking questions, does not force a conclusion, and allows others to draw their own conclusions.[30] Transparency and authenticity manifested through accountability and forgiveness pave a way to reconnect with the world with which the church has lost a once-empathetic touch.

Passionately hating the sin but vigorously loving sinners sets the standard of genuine righteousness. Pursuing a living-sacrifice lifestyle, as specified in Romans 12:1, is a sign of life well lived for Jesus by wearing his coat properly. Thinking about and acting on what Jesus would do in one's given situations requires of him a great deal of sacrifices of interpretation, interpolation, and self-examination.[31]

> Therefore, I urge you, brothers and sisters, in view of God's mercy, to offer your bodies as a living sacrifice, holy and

---

29. Shimron, "New Poll Finds Even Religious Americans Feel the Good Vibrations."
30. Barna Group, "What Makes an Engaging Witness, as Defined by Gen Z."
31. Caputo, *What Would Jesus Deconstruct?*, 24.

> pleasing to God—this is your true and proper worship. (Romans 12:1)

Developing multiplicative small groups of a caring community can also shine Christ's light in a metamodern society of neglect and confusion. Ongoing personal care and an authentic lifestyle can, and will, form cracks in the stony heart of one metamodernist after the other. In a long run, such a lifestyle must influence and eventually lead them to Christ—the true *veritas* they seek.

"Relevancy" is the key word to reach postmodern and metamodern cultures. Some of those who didn't catch relevancy in the church sought out psychics and other similar activities on the rebound. An astonishing number of up to 41 percent of Americans believe in psychics, including 32 percent of "Sunday stalwart" Christians, traditionally the most religious group of all. Forty-two percent of Americans believe that spiritual energy can be located in physical objects. Today, many American Christians have turned to the realms of psychics, spiritual energy, and even reincarnation to satisfy their spiritual hunger and longing.[32] Only the authenticity of genuine Christianity can pull the spiritually contorted folks in the metamodern society. A plain and transparent message, especially on the issue of finances, should be adhered to. It shouldn't be vague but down-to-earth "relevant." No elevated titles of church leadership will impress the metamodern generation. Roles should be signified rather than their titles. Authentic life with narrative preaching can attract them to the churches. "Sunday only" holiness won't push through in a metamodern community. Our ministry approaches ought to be carefully thought through and reprogrammed to be need-sensitive. Also, less burdensome connections with other church members will be ideal to develop a relationship with this self-discovering generation, particularly at the initial stage.

We read a story of Jesus calling Peter to walk on the water in the middle of a storm in Matthew 14:28–33. Even in the storm that surrounded him, Jesus was unintimidated, unbound, and unbroken. As long as Peter put his eyes on Jesus, he also was calm. Together with Jesus, Peter walked on the wavy water amid an intimidating storm, and suddenly the storm became their platform to

---

32. Shimron, "New Poll Finds Even Religious Americans Feel the Good Vibrations."

do the impossible.[33] Metamodernism can be used as our platform to reach the upcoming generations for Christ, for every culture can be either carrier or barrier of the gospel. It all depends on our attitude and strategy. With a missional mindset to contextualize our approaches to impact the forthcoming and challenging culture of metamodernism everywhere, we can win this spiritual war with authentic love for the souls of those for whom Jesus died to redeem.

33. Wilson, *Generation Z*, chapter 1.

PART III

Doing Missions in Difficult Circumstances

7

Mission during Legal Cases

DISCIPLESHIP AND LAWSUIT

Throughout history, the church has prospered through difficult seasons and times. It is the foundational guarantee of Jesus' church: "The gates of Hades will *not* overcome it" (Matthew 16:18, emphasis added). Some of those difficult times are mentioned and elaborated in this section of part III. They're from both my own experience as well as researches made over the years. It is my hope and prayer that readers will find benefits from the following narratives. There may be a time that a missionary needs to carry on fieldwork while he gets involved in the legal case against other believers. You might want to keep in mind that I'm only tackling in this chapter a lawsuit with other Christians. If you're in a legal battle with non-believers, I'll leave that up to your conscience.

It was in mid-2002 that a subpoena came to the Kenyan church leaders whom I mentored for years toward ministry succession. They were sued by a group of individuals who belonged to a partner mission agency and did not wish to see the ministry property relinquished to the local church leadership. We were shocked at first, but the Lord gave us peace and wisdom to deal with the matter onward. The work had to still move on during exhausting court battles that persisted for over a year. Disciples were to be made and churches planted despite the legal case, which ultimately confused many. This is the story of how we overcame the challenge.

Some of the leaders and members feared a possible loss of facilities while others were simply disordered. Our Kenyan disciples were divided into several groups: a group that was readily eager to retaliate in the court, a group that was hurt by this case and didn't want any further trouble (many in this group left for other churches), a group that prayerfully sought the will of the Lord amid the chaos, and a group that was just spectatorial of the circumstances. All of them came into my radar of concern lest I fail them with the biblical discipleship in such a challenging season. While we were aware of the differing interpretations of 1 Corinthians 6:1–8 among Christians, we wanted to hear God's voice and search his heart in his word.

> If any of you has a dispute with another, do you dare to take it before the ungodly for judgment instead of before the Lord's people? Or do you not know that the Lord's people will judge the world? And if you are to judge the world, are you not competent to judge trivial cases? Do you not know that we will judge angels? How much more the things of this life! Therefore, if you have disputes about such matters, do you ask for a ruling from those whose way of life is scorned in the church? I say this to shame you. Is it possible that there is nobody among you wise enough to judge a dispute between believers? But instead, one brother takes another to court—and this in front of unbelievers! The very fact that you have lawsuits among you means you have been completely defeated already. Why not rather be wronged? Why not rather be cheated? Instead, you yourselves cheat and do wrong, and you do this to your brothers and sisters. (1 Corinthians 6:1–8)

I, as a missionary mentor, wanted to implement in my local disciples the biblical application of those verses. My team could have defended ourselves in court as Paul did when he was accused by the Jews in Acts 21:37—23:10. We knew it would have been considered self-defense. However, the most brutal reality was, the local churches under the umbrella of our mission—the body of Christ—were on the brink of a split over this incident. I didn't want to see that. I went over to Africa to build Christ's church, not to divide her. Besides, the name of Christ is often marred and churches are frowned at by ugly court battles engaged by Christians around the world. In fact, someone even consulted his lawyer friend and found out that this kind of lawsuit had nearly a 90 percent chance of a win for the defendant because the plaintiff was mostly composed of foreigners. The case looked favorable to my disciples in multiple ways unless bribery got in the way, which was sporadic in Kenya in those days.

Following the Bible's teaching of Matthew 5:23–25, my disciples and I went to see the plaintiffs and tried to sort things out by talks. We felt that their hearts were as hard as a stone. The plaintiff's demands weren't negotiable—they wanted the property for themselves. When my team realized that our reconciliation attempt was going nowhere, we returned home to no avail. After tiresome meetings with my team, while praying and fasting together, we made a painful decision to inform their lawyer that we'd voluntarily forfeit the rights to the facilities and possessions my team had acquired for those churches.

Soon, there was no longer a basis for the lawsuit. The other party withdrew the case. That was the end of the legal battle. Everyone on the team felt relief from exhaustion as well as sadness from loss. The firestorm was finally gone but with many ashes left behind.[1] Property worth tens of thousands of dollars was lost on our side. The plaintiff group chattered of us that God has condemned us and given them a rightful victory. Most of those who belonged to the spectatorial group left shaking their heads at us. Only a handful of people remained with us.

On the brighter side of this unfortunate crisis, it became easy for us to tell who the genuine disciples and carriers of our vision and mission were. Mostly when we think of the word "crisis," we immediately think of the word "trouble." But a "crisis" can also be viewed differently. One Chinese character for the word "crisis" literally means "dangerous opportunity." It served us as a timely opportunity to sift out those in whom our vision and mission were engraved in their spiritual DNA. Then and only then, we came to realize that it

---

1. Susek, *Firestorm: Preventing and Overcoming Church Conflict*, 65.

was still worth making disciples of the nations. More than anything, the Lord directed my team to keep focusing on making disciples and caring for the remaining leaders and members during this crisis.

Though unpleasant, we willingly left all the property in the plaintiff's hands. The spiritual maturity for my disciples that came along with this unforgettable burn was amazing and graceful. God's word stood out as our guidepost in those somber days. The Lord gave us an obedient heart to his words.

> When they hurled their insults at him, he did not retaliate; when he suffered, he made no threats. Instead, he entrusted himself to him who judges justly. (1 Peter 2:23)

> If it is possible, as far as it depends on you, live at peace with everyone. Do not take revenge, my dear friends, but leave room for God's wrath, for it is written: "It is mine to avenge; I will repay," says the Lord. (Romans 12:18–19)

I know this may sound counter-cultural to those of us who are exposed to a culture familiar with suing mechanism in the United States. America has increasingly become a "blame and sue" society,[2] and many more nations adapted the same particular cultural norm. But I did not go to mission fields to export American culture there. I had to go back to Scripture, the comprehensible and applicable prescription to all mankind, transcending cultures, and see what it says.

> Do everything without grumbling or arguing, so that you may become blameless and pure, "children of God without fault in a warped and crooked generation." Then you will shine among them like stars in the sky as you hold firmly to the word of life. And then I will be able to boast on the day of Christ that I did not run or labor in vain. (Philippians 2:14–16)

Despite feeling a scarred agony inside, my coworkers and I trusted that we were obeying God's word. I've learned a priceless lesson through this incident. When the dust settled, only true friends were left. They stuck around because of vision and mission,

---

2. Williams, "Politics, the Media and Refining the Notion of Fault," 347–54.

since there was scarcely any promise of funding and ministry support left anymore. To put it more precisely, those in whom our vision and mission were planted in their hearts remained. It was a golden opportunity God gave us to start afresh.

A few remaining church leaders regularly met either in my house or at our small rented office. Regularly, we shared a cup of tea and discussed the day's discipleship study topics. If we talked about evangelism, then we'd go out for door-to-door witness on the same day's evening to practice what we learned that day in the study session. We were zealous, and God blessed the sacrificial dedication of our utmost beings. The rebuilding process was on. I discovered through this hard lesson who genuine friends were. Most of those leaders who stood on the foundation of vision and mission became the main engine that runs the African operations of the Evangelical Alliance for Preacher Training/Commission with which I've been gratefully serving as the international director.

TEST OF FORGIVENESS

However, the Lord wanted us to go the extra mile with obedience to his word. On New Year's Eve in the same year of the lawsuit, Eunice and I felt the Lord prompting our hearts to go reconcile further with a former plaintiff. I was inclined to deny his prompting at first because it was certainly going against my human nature to bless the accusers. Nevertheless, we strongly sensed that he really wanted us to do this, so we decided to obey. On the morning of New Year's Day, we bought a gift and went to see the family of a former plaintiff. Eunice and I presented our gift as a token of full reconciliation and blessed them. As we were leaving their quarter, I could undoubtedly feel the Lord smiling on us and tapping me on the shoulder with "Well done." God's presence was so real that day.

Something else happened from then on. Some of my disciples passing by the area that day accidentally saw us leaving the former plaintiff's quarter and asked us later what we were doing there. We shared the story, and it was spread and somehow sparked the notion of forgiveness among my team. Upon hearing the story, everyone experienced the power of forgiveness and healing from the court incident. The church was founded upon God's forgiveness through Christ. Churches and ministries in our mission began to see unprecedented growth once we learned to forgive. It was as if God was opening a faucet of his blessing and releasing exponential multiplication afterward. The vision was rekindled upon the biblical foundation of forgiveness. The Lord taught me and my African coworkers a priceless and imperative lesson of dealing prudently with possible quarrels in church ministry.

Besides, crisis reveals our leadership characters. Whether we know it or not, people are watching us more keenly in crisis. This is another invaluable lesson I learned through this experience. Afterward, many more new church facilities were acquired by God's grace, and the mission expanded from Kenya to ten other African nations and even beyond Africa later. We felt God rewarding us for our obedience to the biblical principle over legal cases among Christians.

Unfortunately, it isn't uncommon to see court battles between Christians over the church and mission properties across the world in this time and age. Should you be put into this unfortunate dilemma of a legal battle, you're advised to obey the instructions of God's word and trust the Holy Spirit to do his work while putting your best effort into the discipleship of the people you've gone to serve on the mission field. In Genesis chapter 1, we discover that everything God created was of good quality (Genesis 1:4, 10, 12, 18, 21, 25). So should everything we do in God's missions. However, what God did with the creation and redemption of mankind was of the best quality (Genesis 1:31; John 3:16). So should our work of discipleship of people God has called us to serve. This thought will direct your path if you find yourself in an unfortunate legal battle with other believers while following Christ in his unstoppable mission.

8

Mission in Political Unrest and Natural Calamity

NATIONS IN UPROAR

> For the transgression of a land many are the princes thereof: but by a man of understanding and knowledge the state thereof shall be prolonged. (Proverbs 28:2, KJV)

When greed and corruption infiltrate the princes of a nation, the nation can drive the people of the land into agony and suffering. In extreme cases, chaos may creep into a political realm, and the tranquility of the land gets jeopardized. Many were shocked at the news of a missionary group abducted in Haiti by a heavily armed Mawozo gang after visiting an orphanage in Croix-des-Bouquets in October 2021.[1] Regrettably, there are political upheavals, if not wars, in troubled regions of the earth in almost every generation. Yet, our Lord's charge to go and make disciples of *all nations* continues to beckon his body to do missions both in peaceful season and turbulent season. If you or your loved ones are serving the

---

1. Dube and Montes, "Group of 16 Americans and a Canadian, Including Five Children, Kidnapped in Haiti."

Lord and happen to be placed in a difficult context of disturbance or disaster, this chapter is for you.

> You will hear of wars and rumors of wars, but see to it that you are not alarmed. Such things must happen, but the end is still to come. Nation will rise against nation, and kingdom against kingdom. (Matthew 24:6–7a)

SAME OLD QUESTION

I'm writing this chapter from the perspective of a cross-cultural missionary where he has to deal with political elections on the mission field as a foreigner as well as a spiritual leader. It's not my intention to get into debates here as to how far a missionary should get involved in local politics. If you're a missionary, local people do consider you as a religious leader and sometimes wish to get your opinions on their local politics, especially when the election season is around the corner. As my missionary work was based in four different countries in the past, I've been regularly asked by my students, disciples, and congregants during election seasons: "Which candidate do you endorse?," "Who do you think is the candidate God has appointed for such a time as this?," "If you were a Kenyan (or a Korean or a Filipino) citizen, who would you have voted for?" . . . the list goes on.

To this same question with many variations, my answer was always fixed: "Christians are to carefully and prayerfully cast their votes for someone who possesses godly character and pursues godly leadership." With the full period there, it is normally where I drew the line between my professionalism and my individual preferences. Personally, I never shared with anyone outside of my family about my voting choices. I was aware that God had put me in an influential position for a reason, and such a privilege must be used always with caution to bless others, not to favor my preferences or harness my gain.

Of course, a missionary must remind and educate his local disciples and followers to prayerfully discern and vote for a political candidate with godly motivation and leadership. A godly leader is relational and sacrificial, is not manipulative, and serves by lowering himself and elevating others. On the other hand, an ungodly leader exploits, manipulates, enslaves, and elevates himself by stamping on others.

> Be shepherds of God's flock that is under your care, watching over them—not because you must, but because you are willing, as God wants you to be; not pursuing dishonest gain, but eager to serve. (1 Peter 5:2)

> In fact, you even put up with anyone who enslaves you or exploits you or takes advantage of you or puts on airs or slaps you in the face. (2 Corinthians 11:20)

> I am the good shepherd. The good shepherd lays down his life for the sheep. The hired hand is not the shepherd and does not own the sheep. So when he sees the wolf coming, he abandons the sheep and runs away. Then the wolf attacks the flock and scatters it. The man runs away because he is a hired hand and cares nothing for the sheep. (John 10:11–13)

Whenever the election season draws near, Christian leaders are responsible to provide godly instructions about voting and electing political leaders. Christians should be reminded to put aside their personal inclinations and look into the biblical guidelines to select a man or woman after God's heart. First Samuel 16:7 reminds us not to consider the political candidate's appearance or his/her status but the heart, as the Lord does not look at the things people look at. A Christian voter should cast a precious vote toward the leader who is mindful of the common good of the citizens. The Bible talks plenty about such guidelines.

KINGDOM IDENTITY AND PERSONAL IDENTITY

In some cultures, politics are more intertwined with religious life. Then things may be a bit tricky. We need to deeply think about the missionary's identity and cost of discipleship in line with the instruction of Luke 14:26–33.

> If anyone comes to me and does not hate father and mother, wife and children, brothers and sisters—yes, even their own life—such a person cannot be my disciple. And whoever does not carry their cross and follow me cannot be my disciple. Suppose one of you wants to build a tower. Won't you first sit down and estimate the cost to see if you have enough money to complete it? For if you lay the foundation and are not able to finish it, everyone who sees it will ridicule you, saying, "This person began to build and wasn't able to finish." Or suppose a king is about to go to war against another king. Won't he first sit down and consider whether he is able with ten thousand men to oppose the one coming against him with twenty thousand? If he is not able, he will send a delegation while the other is still a long way off and will ask for terms of peace. In the same way, those of you who do not give up everything you have cannot be my disciples.

When we respond to Christ's call of discipleship, Jesus becomes our king. This means we're his subjects. There has been the transfer of ownership. We can't persist in "me-first" faith anymore. Jesus' kingdom identity comes first before our personal identities. God's children are first and foremost called to be allegiant to the Father's kingdom before they're allegiant to their nationalities, clans, political views, and so forth. "My kingdom is not of this world," Jesus said (John 18:36). The same goes for us—Christ's followers. Christians represent God, whether they like it or not. In a sense, every Christian is a public figure. Thus, in my opinion, it is generally not wise for a missionary to side with any political candidate, tribe, and party during the sensitive election periods unless God clearly speaks to him/her otherwise. Please remember: Missionaries' words are counted in many cases, especially to their local followers. They may need to choose their politics-related words always carefully.

OVERCOMING STORIES IN UNRESTS

> I have told you these things, so that in me you may have peace. In this world you will have trouble. But take heart! I have overcome the world. (John 16:33)

It was December of 2007 when Mwai Kibaki was swiftly sworn in as the reelected president of Kenya by claiming a come-from-behind win in one of the tightest presidential races in Kenyan history. There was no colorful ceremony at a city central park, celebrated by a massive crowd, like before in 2002. The opposition leader and his followers didn't yield to the election result in suspicion of rigging in the vote-counting process. As was often the case in other countries in modern history, the prolonged court battle over disputed election results was linked to the proliferated nationwide ethnic clashes because both the ruling party and the opposition party were dominantly represented by certain ethnic groups. Extreme segregation and violent assaults followed after the court nullified the opposition party's complaint. Along with continued blame games, angry mobs raided homes and properties of people from other ethnicities. Thousands lost their lives and hundreds of thousands were displaced from their homes to become refugees in their own country. Violence and killings swept the streets. It was one unforgettable testing period for everyone in this East African nation.

As we were heading to our mission school one day, we saw human bodies lying and blood flowing through drainages on the street. They must have been slaughtered the night before. It was one of the most horrific sights we could never forget. Eunice and I once thought about leaving the country temporarily until the situation calmed down. Yet, after much prayer and consideration, my family decided to stay and provide emotional and material help to our church leaders and members who were affected by the clash. Closely monitoring the news on both media and on-the-ground stories from church members, we managed to be there for them during the difficult time for our local followers and for Kenya at large. Looking back, God's grace was prevalent in many aspects.

Throughout this national disorder, we constantly reminded the local church pastors in our mission not to side with any tribe or political party in their public ministry appeals. People should be able to reflect God, not a certain tribe or party, when they see a pastor or missionary, we believed. One study shows that 64 percent of practicing Christians and 44 percent of all US adults believe that churches have a significant role to address and improve ethnic reconciliations.[2] The same goes for many other nations. Most of our churches were spared from tribal assaults during the stormy season because our local pastors stayed on their primary call to foster God's kingdom and preach nothing other than his word.

There is another overcoming story of God's people in political unrest. It is a story of "D," a female teacher who worked at one of the kindergartens Eunice led in Kenya. As mentioned earlier, Africa is infamous for its ethnic tension and political violence during the time of election campaigns and the ensuing tally of votes. Sometimes political gangs are mobilized and paid to arouse such turmoil. It was a campaign season in Nairobi, the capital of Kenya. The general election was to be held around the corner. Together with her friends, let's just say, D was passing by the wrong section of the town at the wrong time. Suddenly, a political mob surrounded the ladies and gang-raped them. To make matters worse, the other lady who accompanied D was later diagnosed with AIDS, infected by one of the rapists. Although D wasn't infected by the HIV virus, she soon learned that she was pregnant. In the following days and weeks, D suffered trauma from the incident. She was getting shriveled day by day. Rightfully so: the seed of her enemy was growing in her womb.

Eunice provided personal counseling over a period of six months to help D recover from trauma. D's greatest fear was to be reminded of her perpetuators' face whenever she'd look at the baby and, at the worst, that she would have to put up with that for the rest of her life. Thanks to the spiritual nurture and physical care of the Christian community around her, D slowly found her peace. Despite the pressures from her non-Christian relatives who urged D to secretly undergo an abortion, she firmly decided to keep the baby. God was still working in the heart of D. We witnessed her

---

2. For an exhaustive research on this subject, see Barna Group, *Beyond Diversity*.

heal and mature during this time of turbulence while the baby was growing in her womb for the next nine months.

On the day of her delivery, the mother wasn't able to deliver the baby by normal birth due to D's emotional stress and physical condition. The baby wasn't even placed in her womb in a normal position for safe delivery. The doctor ordered an urgent Cesarean delivery lest the life of both mother and baby be endangered and the complication be prolonged. Finally, when the baby was delivered, it was a girl. To everyone's surprise, D confessed that she couldn't see a single trace of her perpetuators on the face of the baby. The baby was but her own child given to her by God's blessing. D named the baby "Blessing," literally. We were marveled at this miracle God had performed in D's life. Everyone who heard D's story was utterly amazed at the power of God's forgiveness and restoration. God has even used a ministry partner in England to help finance D's delivery costs and hospital bills with a donation. It was our sheer joy to watch Blessing grow under the loving care of D until we left Kenya years later. Today, D is a minister, serving in the church planted right in the area where she was once victimized. Her life continues to reflect Christ's gospel of forgiveness and to write a beautiful story of God's irresistible grace of restoration by reaching out to someone who may likewise need the message of hope.

Many years later in February 2021, other news was decorating the international newspaper headlines—the Myanmar coup. It was right after that I received an urgent message from "M," one of the Burmese students who was taking a course in my online class. She was previously cut off from all communications, so I was getting worried. She somehow managed to get temporary internet access and explained the ground situation to me. The nation just went under an indefinite-term state of emergency. The military group detained the president and other leaders and cut off the wi-fi, internet, and all landline connections. Soon, all social media was banned to put the country under easy control of the militant group. The following months continued with the news of citizen protests and military killings on the streets. Fearing the impending arrest and assault of young leaders in the town, desperate M fled in the middle of the night, made it to the nearest border, and crossed over to India. While she was on the run, she shared the gospel with people she met on the road and kept leading them to Christ. In the refugee camp where she stayed, she planted a church with those she discipled in faith along the journey. God was still working through M to shine the light of his gospel in another stark and forbidding region of this world. The enemy meant to harm her has been turned around by God to accomplish the good of saving many souls. Joseph's confession is repeatedly echoed in history by those who held onto Christ and relied on his power to overcome the darkness of unrest and war with the light of the gospel:

> You intended to harm me, but God intended it for good to accomplish what is now being done, the saving of many lives. (Genesis 50:20)

AID, FEAR, AND DISCIPLESHIP

To do the missions right during social unrest, one has to deal with the two greatest needs of provision and peace. War is often accompanied by food shortage, looting, rape, displacement, and separation from the family.[3] Someone once told me that a Chinese letter for "peace" consists of the characters meaning food, mouth, and "to level." Indeed, peace is made possible when food is evenly shared with all mouths. I also heard this expression one day from one of our church leaders I met in Moshi, Tanzania, when I was ministering there: *Food is about dignity. There is no human dignity without adequate food.* No matter who they are, hungry people ought to be fed. Jesus would do so (Matthew 14:13–21; 15:32–39; Mark 6:31–44; 8:1–9; Luke 9:12–17; John 6:1–14). Access to food is the basic right of human beings, the image of God. If a missionary is in a position to help, he is much encouraged to assist the need of the community by feeding the hungry among the war victims.

Next, a missionary will need to tackle the issue of fear in the hearts of his local followers. There could be both internal and external influxes of volatility endangering social tranquility during any kind of political unrest. Many studies have been made on the

---

3. Kighoma, *Church and Mission in the Context of War*, chapter 1.

subject of biblical *shalom* as well as suggestions for an exhibition of such godly characteristics in organizations and communities. Should a missionary decide to stay with the local people during unrest and war, he'd direly need the sense of the presence of Jesus, the Prince of Peace, transcending the surrounding dangers and risks. Amid the atmosphere of insecurity and agitation, a spiritual shepherd must know how to tame the anxious self and his followers and to minister God's word to everyone circumspectly.

> And the peace of God, which transcends all understanding, will guard your hearts and your minds in Christ Jesus. (Philippians 4:7)

If a missionary decides to evacuate and stay away from the area for any reason during unrest and war, working on a communication channel will be of absolute need. Regular check-ups and constant monitoring of the field situation should be maintained remotely. Individual and corporate intercession for the local believers' safety is essential. Not only for the sake of following the biblical mandate of discipleship but also for the continuation of the work in absence of missionaries on the field, your goal is to raise local coworkers and successors from day one of your field life. This will prevent discontinuation of the precious ministry God has started through you in case of inevitable evacuation or forced expulsion. Jean Johnson talks of how missionaries should concentrate on planting an indigenous church that is led by local leaders as soon as they arrive on the mission field. She asserts that we should plant churches as if there "will be a coup d'etat any day."[4] We're to let the Holy Spirit disciple and mature the local successors through us because his work is afoot from the moment we meet a local person in the mission field.

In case God leads you to minister in a dire situation related to social unrest and war, it is advised to seek to meet the practical needs of aid and fear among the victims. Discipleship shouldn't be overlooked in the meantime because that is the heart of the Great Commission. Guiding and nurturing the believers on the

---

4. Johnson, "Why We Should Plant Churches as If There Will be a Coup D'état Any Day," 4–6.

versability of forgiveness equally matures them toward the fullness of Christ (Ephesians 4:13).

ETHNIC AVERSION

This world has been continuously ailing due to civil unrest and political wars of both small and large scales throughout history. The Bible affirms that causes of conflict vary from insufficiency, greed, selfishness, comparison, misunderstanding, and even to satanic promotion. James 4:1–2 points out on this issue:

> What causes fights and quarrels among you? Don't they come from your desires that battle within you? You desire but do not have, so you kill. You covet but you cannot get what you want, so you quarrel and fight. You do not have because you do not ask God.

In the same context, there are people who hold an aversion to certain groups of people and turn their bigotry and hatred into an excuse to oppress others for profits. From the Middle East to Africa, the historical atrocity of genocide and ethnic cleansing traces its root to this ethnic aversion. This ungodly cause recurrently triggers assault and violence. The Black Lives Matter movement was initially formed in response to the acquittal of George Zimmerman[5] and later became a sensation in the United States and around the world at the death of George Floyd in 2020.[6] Though controversial about some of their tactics, protests of the movement centered on the reform of systemic anti-Black racism in society. At the outbreak of the COVID-19 pandemic that was believed to have emerged in Wuhan, China,[7] hate crimes against Asians skyrocketed across America by those making a sweeping denunciation of fellow Americans of all Asian heritages.[8]

---

5. Lebron, *The Making of Black Lives Matter*, 151.

6. Sobo et al., "More Than a Teachable Moment," 243–48.

7. Lin et al., "A Conceptual Model for the Coronavirus Disease 2019 (COVID-19) Outbreak in Wuhan, China, with Individual Reaction and Governmental Action," 211–16.

8. Gover et al., "Anti-Asian Hate Crime during the COVID-19 Pandemic," 647–67.

Ethnic aversion (or "racism," as some may call it) is a sin problem. It goes much deeper than skin colors or cultural differences.[9] Forgiveness and acceptance are at the core of the gospel message. Genuine heart transmission of the gospel can cure us from the sin of ethnic aversion and racism. Churches and Christians in the melting pot society of America in particular have a role to play as peacemakers in resolving barriers and hate between races and ethnicities. Joshua Glasgow wittily suggests in his philosophical view that race is simply not real or it could be real only in the basic sense. In his argument, the concept of racism has just a meaningless basis. While there are differences of people in biological senses, Glasgow has made a point to see people as just people.[10] After all, the problem is discrimination of people and people groups on the basis of any personal difference, not the difference itself. In Christ and in his reconciliatory message of the gospel, we can, and must, find the cure for ethnic aversion and its root issue. It has to start from the church.

REALITY OF CALAMITY

> There will be *famines* and *earthquakes* in various places. All these are the beginning of birth pains. (Matthew 24:7b–8, emphasis added)

In 1960, the Institute for Economics and Peace recorded thirty-nine natural disasters on the planet. Less than sixty years later in 2019, the number showed a skyrocketed figure of 396. The global number of natural disasters has increased by ten times. The below data shows that a dramatic rise has been recorded in the global number of catastrophic natural events in the last century.[11]

---

9. Anderson, *Gracism*, 18.
10. See Glasgow et al., *What Is Race*.
11. Vision of Humanity, "Increase in Natural Disasters on a Global Scale by Ten Times." Used with permission.

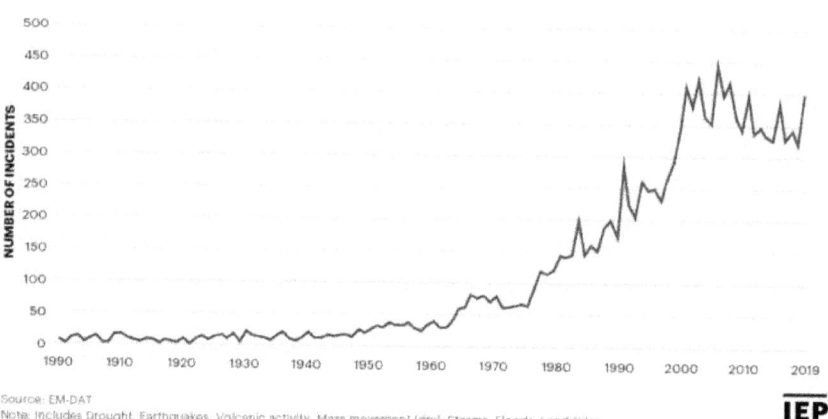

Figure 2. Increase of Natural Disasters Worldwide

Natural disasters affected 2.9 billion people globally from 2000 to 2012 and caused damage of $1.7 trillion. In 2017, a total of sixteen natural disasters hit American soil and recorded a peak of $300 billion in damage in that year alone. Each disaster cost the US at least $1 billion.[12] When a calamity or natural disaster hits the community, it is quite common that more people scurry to God than at other times. Many seek a channel to connect with God in the sense of emergency. Their spiritual interest often dies out when the damage gets restored and the dust settles, one may argue. Yet, the body of Christ should not let such open doors slip by, failing to make contact with hurting ones in the community at the very point of their needs.[13]

Besides, the Bible talks about the possible calamity of various kinds everywhere as we get nearer to the Lord's return. As a missionary on call to prepare for his return by fulfilling the Great Commission, sometimes we might well encounter calamity on our way. Several suggestions are expounded here on how to behave and minister effectively should such calamities unexpectedly come

---

12. Wilson, *Generation Z*, chapter 1.
13. McNeal, *The Present Future*, 5.

to meet us on our paths. Whether you're a victim yourself or you know victims around you or both you and others are co-victims of the calamity, you can find helping hands in such dire situations by acting out of wisdom and prudency. Here is another anecdote about how we have overcome such a challenging situation in our own experience.

In November 2020, Typhoon Ulysses hit Manila, Philippines. I woke up early in the morning at the loud knocks of a neighbor on my house gate. My neighbors were warning us that the nearby Marikina River overflowed and the water level rose to submerge our cars parked outside the house. My family and I were helplessly watching the water level encroach by the minute, almost entering into our living room. It was a devastating sight to watch. My family and I had to eventually evacuate the house for a time, with a prayer that God would stop the rain lest the water level continues to rise.

To make the matter worse, it was during the time of global pandemic and community lockdown. In real missions, difficulties meet missionaries on the road in packages more or less, which make them even more distressing. When such chaos bumps into your life without an appointment, this Bible verse usually speaks louder: "One who has unreliable friends soon comes to ruin, but there is a friend who sticks closer than a brother" (Proverbs 18:24). This is an important factor to consider in a life emergency. Due to the time-sensitive nature of the matter, having someone near you to aid your need is far more efficient if the calamity hits you. Get emergency helps from a nearby missionary or local person just as Proverbs 27:10 confirms: "Do not forsake your friend or a friend of your family, and do not go to your relative's house when disaster strikes you—better a neighbor nearby than a relative far away." Also, extend your help to them. Reaching out to the immediate need of your neighbors can open an additional door to share the gospel with them. Your warm gesture of extending a helping hand by providing shelter, phone charge, free wi-fi, or even just a cup of water will be remembered by your neighbors for a long time. It will be one watershed moment for Christians and churches to build relationships with the community after all.

GIVING OF RELIEF AIDS

Though relief aid giving is knit tightly with the nature of urgency and necessity, the issue of stewardship can't be overlooked here. The significance of a transparent and faster channel to provide relief aids in calamity needs to be addressed. When it comes to your giving through governmental organizations, a forethought on the issue of stewardship may be in order because of the lack of follow-up and record-tracing systems often detected in their giving channels. In some developing countries and organizations within, sometimes your intended aid may not be reaching the very people you wish to help with imminent needs owing to corruption and greed of officials who wish to take advantage of the misfortune of others. Some may cut a portion of the entire amount as their own claimed "commission fees." However, if the Lord prompts your heart to extend your hand through the particular channel, you might as well just bite the bullet and be of immediate help to the victims in any way you can.

Otherwise, it'll be better to give through a channel of people that either you know or you can follow up with. If you know someone involved in such areas, who is directly involved and is already on the ground in administrating and touching the locals to disburse the aid effectively and timely, the channel will be far more stewardship-oriented to give through. You can also disburse your aid through validated churches and organizations that are reaching out to the disaster victims. It'll be certainly good stewardship to direct your giving for this noble cause through trustworthy agencies.

You're encouraged to be mindful of not only the giving channel but also the end result of your giving. While aiding the victims directly or indirectly, it'll be good to remember that you're an agent of peace in stewarding conflicts. Christians are called to be peacemakers by promoting unity and love even through giving. Your giving shouldn't result in quarrels and division. It ought to aim to produce a constructive result. Above all, seeking an opportunity to glorify God, serve others, and become more like Christ will be the ultimate goal.

9

Mission during Pandemic

DOUBLE DILEMMA

While it was globally affecting almost everyone on earth, the latest COVID-19 challenge has put cross-cultural gospel workers abroad into a greater dilemma mostly due to the poor medical conditions they were exposed to in developing countries. Some missionaries evacuated the field while others stayed on. Both had to go through what they've not encountered before in the unique situation of a global pandemic.[1]

Those who returned home faced reentry culture shocks almost with no preparation because they abruptly evacuated the field. Some of them even had to pay for house rents both in their home country and field country. Many believed the pandemic would end soon and would return to their field assignments in no time, so they rented a temporary lodging at home while they kept their residences on the field, intending to return soon. They never expected that the duration would be prolonged up to years when one country after another began to close their borders to foreigners to stop the international spread of the deadly disease. This delay stalled them and even forced some to decide to stay at home for

---

1. Hopkins, "For Expats and Missionaries, COVID-19 Was a Crossroads."

other ministry calls. Meantime, a number of supporting churches financially struggled due to a drop in church attendance and giving as well during the lockdown. It has affected missions giving and eventually financially hurt missionaries both on the field and at home.

A part of the dilemma surrounded the decision-making process of whether or not they needed to leave or stay on the field. Barry Johnson's polarity management model was utilized by some mission agencies to help determine their field missionaries to make proper moves pertaining to this sensitive issue.[2]

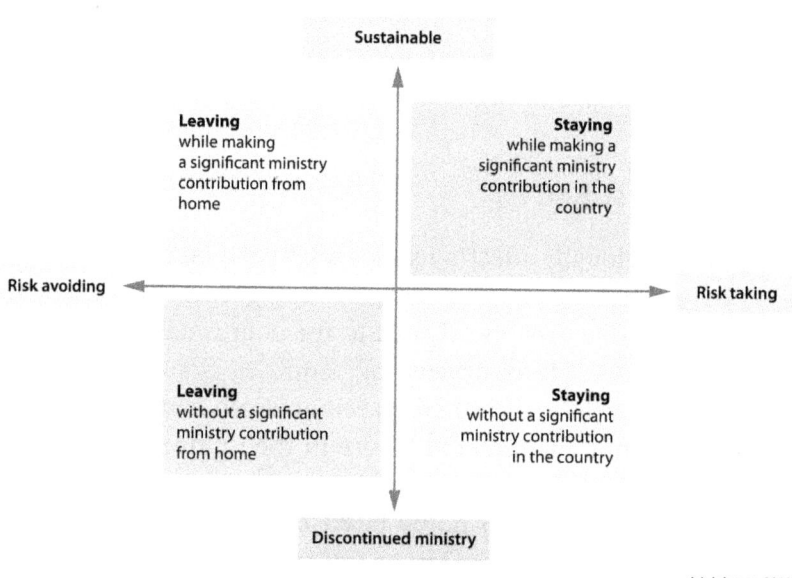

Figure 3. Polarity Management Model

The COVID-19 pandemic has further triggered the development of risk-handling models in missionary bodies. A need to analyze situations, not with an irresponsible attitude of avoidance but with an accountable attitude of servant-stewardship, arose amid the crisis. On top of utilizing Johnson's risk-handling model, a missionary must be mindful of making a decision that would not cause his local followers to stumble in their faith (Matthew

2. Johnson, *Polarity Management*, 79–96. Used with permission.

5:29–30; 18:6–9; Mark 9:42–47; Luke 17:2; Romans 14:21). Loving treatment and bonding connection during crisis leave a strong impression and can heavily affect the missionary's discipleship effort for the long term. Healthy models to sustain the ministry with or without the missionary presence were also suggested. The issues of encouraging local ownership and intentional mentoring toward succession to local leadership were raised all over again.[3]

NOT UNPRECEDENTED

The recent COVID-19 pandemic took millions of lives worldwide. As alarming as it has been, with its global impact, the pandemic isn't unprecedented at all. In biblical times, there were pandemics. The Bible calls it "pestilence" or "plague" and mentions it over fifty times. In Leviticus 13, we find strict quarantine regulations for those who suffered perilous diseases along with detailed diagnosis and hygienic protocols. God is more mindful of epidemics or pandemics in human society than most of us think. This shows that our God is not distant from human affairs, as alleged by deists. He is deeply involved in day-to-day human life, including epidemics and pandemics.

"Pandemic" isn't an alien term to human history. When the Spanish flu hit Europe at the beginning of the twentieth century, the virus was spreading exponentially throughout the continent. What did the body of Christ do in that devastating time? Throughout history, one society after another witnessed the beauty of Christ when Christians demonstrated love and extended care toward their neighbors. The glory of Christ shone brighter each time the church extended to be the hands and feet of Christ for the hurting and needy ones. Such expressions of Christian love scarcely failed to result in greater evangelism in the communities when the crisis was over.

In 165 AD, a plague devastated the Roman Empire, killing one of three citizens of the time.[4] It happened again in 249 AD, which shriveled the mighty Roman Empire with a dramatic population

---

3. Rievan, "In a Pandemic, Should Missionaries Leave or Stay?"
4. Bruun, "The Antonine Plague and the 'Third-century Crisis,'" 201–17.

drop owing to countless deaths. The Roman government helplessly sought out a solution but was defeated with none except growing numbers of Christians who bravely stood alongside communities to care for the sick and needy.[5] Suffering under rampant persecution of the day, Christians would have sneered at the empire with a jeering claim of divine judgment on them through plagues. Yet their response was different. They came up with care and love for neighbors, often their persecutors. Water, food, and friendship were nurtured at the sickbed. In fact, if you had a Christian friend, you would have had a better chance of surviving the plague. Christians shone the light of Christ in the dark crises of pandemics in the past. They selflessly did so simply by believing that they have served Christ himself when they cared for others.

It took only two hundred years for the Christian population of the early church to grow from 0.07 percent to 52.9 percent in the Roman Empire. This is heavily credited to the overwhelming cares of Christians during difficult times of history. It ultimately led the empire to end Christian persecution and open a door to its Christianization.[6] David Mathis pointed out, "Christ's church will endure and shine out all the clearer. Hard times are good days to be Christian."[7] The soils of people's hearts usually become softened and turn more approachable during pandemics than usual times. Souls are extra receptive to the sharing of Christ's love and gospel message and, in turn, ripe for harvest.

NOT FORSAKING THE ASSEMBLY?

> Not forsaking the assembling of ourselves together, as is the manner of some, but exhorting one another, and so much the more as you see the Day approaching. (Hebrews 10:25, NKJV)

The impact of global lockdowns was felt mostly on gathering capacity, and it heavily affected the regular assembly of the churches

---

5. Cameron, *The Later Roman Empire*, 10.
6. Brockman and Habito, *The Gospel among Religions*, 7–15.
7. Mathis, "Corona Cannot Prevail against Her."

worldwide. In the sixteenth century when another deadly plague hit Europe, Martin Luther, a Protestant Reformer, wrote a letter to his friend about how the church should behave in such complicated situations. I believe Luther's principle still rings true today. Reading through his letter might be helpful for us to act balanced at the critical juncture of pandemics and epidemics. He wrote:

> What else is the epidemic but a fire which instead of consuming wood and straw devours life and body? You ought to think this way: Very well, by God's decree the enemy has sent us poison and deadly offal. Therefore I shall ask God mercifully to protect us. Then I shall fumigate, help purify the air, administer medicine, and take it. I shall avoid places and persons where my presence is not needed in order not to become contaminated and thus perchance infect and pollute others, and so cause their death as a result of my negligence. If God should wish to take me, he will surely find me and I have done what he has expected of me and so I am not responsible for either my own death or the death of others. If my neighbor needs me, however, I shall not avoid place or person but will go freely . . . See, this is such a God-fearing faith because it is neither brash nor foolhardy and does not tempt God.[8]

Yes, the pandemic is a spiritual issue, but it also regards the physical dimension. I do not deem it healthy to hyper-spiritualize everything. Surely, we must reach out to those in need as much as we can, but with necessary caution. The Lord will give you wisdom and love both as a godly leader of God's church and a good citizen of the community. Even if a pastor calls for a temporary closure of services or momentarily transfers into house church meetings in smaller units to honor social distancing policy, I don't believe it to be a cowardly act. It may take even more courage for a pastor to make the painful decision of the temporary cease of Sunday assemblies despite knowing the expected drop of tithes and offerings and a likely scenario of limited church outreaches in the long haul. We need pastors with gentle shepherding hearts who look after both the spiritual and physical welfare of their flock.

---

8. Luther, "Whether One May Flee from a Deadly Plague," 113–38.

With this in mind, most churches and mission agencies turned their ministry format into a digitalized platform during the COVID-19 pandemic. Many international meetings, which would have previously cost thousands of dollars and days of travel time, were held via Zoom and other similar video conferencing apps from the comfort of their living rooms. The development of online technology has opened a new door of opportunity. It was indisputably accelerated during the COVID-19 pandemic that affected the globe, and so were the online communication tools and learning management systems. Bible colleges and seminaries likewise saw great potential for campus expansion without walls and borders through online education tools. Rightfully, another definition of BC and AD were added as a result of enhanced home-based lifestyle: "before coronavirus" and "after domestication."

Although pandemic wasn't unprecedented in history, the generalization of virtual meeting technology was. It has somehow extended the meaning of ἐκκλησία (*ecclesia*, or "church" in Greek) and presumably more so in the post-COVID era. It was meant to be contextualized afresh. Thus, the new face of a post-COVID church may want to focus on how many parishioners are *connected* with the leadership and one another (either in-person or virtually) rather than how many of them show up on Sundays. It'll be a whole new dimension Christian leaders may well have to tackle in the post-COVID world.

However, a downside of online ministry was also witnessed. Many churches turned to online worship and Zoom Bible study during the COVID-19 pandemic. In the first several months, most churches seemed to have gained more worshippers in the number of online visitors. After some time, however, most churches complained about a dramatic decrease in online worshippers. Barna research indicated that 50 percent of millennial churchgoers, 35 percent of Gen X churchgoers, and 26 percent of baby-boomer churchgoers stopped attending online worship during the pandemic.[9] Thom Rainer listed reasons for declining online church worship attendance, and they were mainly summarized as (1)

---

9. Hudson, "Millennials Have Stopped Attending Online Church."

diminished curiosity, (2) divided focus between digital and in-person services, and (3) lack of resources, clarity, and vision.[10]

While it's true that the pandemic introduced alternative ways to do church ministries, we shouldn't forget that online worship is but a tool that helps us link with the subsequential steps of human touch. Some people might have lived in a virtual world too long (or too deep) to the point of forgetting the palpable benefits of personal tangibility. In most cases in history, it was the vibrant small groups that helped survive and even thrive the spiritual wellbeing of their members during pandemics and epidemics. Many small groups not only followed safety guidelines and met regularly but also provided adhesive care, interpersonal bonding, and a key to doing the mission right during the pandemic.

For instance, there is a beautiful story of a church plant in New York, which started in March 2020, just before the pandemic hit the area. This newly planted church shifted to a small group care system to cope with meeting the needs of members who found difficulty in the pandemic. Instead of using tithes and offerings to run the status quo of church maintenance, leaders of the new church decided to distribute the fund to help the poor. Even after the pandemic in the US began to head downhill, the church was determined to carry the same ministry forward beyond the pandemic. They believed God has used COVID-19 to shape the church to pursue the call to minister to those that suffer. "We are a church born in suffering for those who experience suffering," Pastor Jason James of New Hope Church stated.[11]

New Hope Church demonstrated what the church is meant to be in the middle of a community crisis. Online services were utilized as a means to connect church members to share their needs. The Body of Christ is called to reach out to the poor and needy regardless of time and place. She should find a way to do exactly that even in pandemics. That will make the church stand out as the salt and light in the darkness of a pandemic, just as she is called to be.

---

10. Rainer, "Seven Reasons Your Online Worship Attendance Is Declining."

11. Lea, "How One NY Church Plant Launched March 1 and Did More Than Just Survive 2020."

> You are the salt of the earth. But if the salt loses its saltiness, how can it be made salty again? It is no longer good for anything, except to be thrown out and trampled underfoot. You are the light of the world. A town built on a hill cannot be hidden. Neither do people light a lamp and put it under a bowl. Instead they put it on its stand, and it gives light to everyone in the house. In the same way, let your light shine before others, that they may see your good deeds and glorify your Father in heaven. (Matthew 5:13–16)

DOING A MISSION VIRTUALLY

The prolonged COVID-19 pandemic put most parts of the world under lockdown for extended periods. As new mutations are found every couple of weeks, scientists predict that the impact of COVID will stay with us and circulate around the world for the next few years.[12] Nations will be required to come up with their own protective means and public health protocols to deal with uprising situations. The world as we know it has changed after COVID-19. The face of missions also changed. While some countries in the First World may get an expedited development of vaccines and secure enough of them for their citizens, many other countries in the Two-Thirds World are prone to suffer devastating consequences still in the years to come. Deeply politicized through corruption, donated and purchased vaccines from one nation to others may not adequately reach the citizens of the Two-Thirds World. Anti-Christian bigotry would be rampantly practiced in COVID economic aid distribution worldwide. While a few countries may enjoy the day when COVID will be in their rear-view mirror, most countries will still have to wrestle through it right in front of their windshield. While the vaccines would not provide 100 percent protection from the coronavirus, the polarity of vaccine distribution is still to vulnerably reflect the nation's economy and political influence. Since we may not see privatization of vaccine

---

12. Lovelace Jr., "Americans Will Need Masks Indoors as US Heads for 'Dangerous Fall' with Surge in Delta Covid Cases."

distribution anytime soon, moves of global missionary forces will also be affected by the origin of the missionary and vaccine distribution of the country. While on long-term and short-term mission trips, there are still many sensitive COVID-related protocols that missionaries need to be mindful of—perhaps not for you if you're fully vaccinated, but for many local ministry counterparts who might have not been granted the vaccination opportunity.

It should be also noted that the COVID-related lockdown in the United States was somewhat different from the rest of the world. In some states, it was barely a lockdown with a minimal period of home stay. To others, it was an extended quarantine that caused emotional fatigue and mental drain. While the new normal is setting its pace at a lower level, vaccination and lockdown were more than medical issues to some people. Cultural and historical circumstances were additionally tied to them. COVID-19 and vaccination have been dealt with more as ideology and politics. It is unfortunate that people have sorted themselves out in the churches during and beyond the pandemic period. Many people changed or left a church over COVID issues. One out of six vaccinated Americans did not share their COVID vaccination history with some of their anti-vaxxer family and friends out of fear of alienation from them, while one out of seventeen didn't tell anyone about it.[13] I'm aware that there are people who wished to remain unvaccinated for various reasons while they have access to vaccination around. While I respect their choices, it is advised for them to be mindful of the global situations owing to the vaccine shortage. If you happen to be one of them and wish to go for a short-term or long-term mission trip, you might want to try not to offend the unvaccinated local people because it won't be easy for most of them to understand your stand. You'd certainly not want to put a stumbling block with your vaccination choice before people whose souls you went to save.

Missio Nexus made a survey in 2020 with 141 mission agencies, churches, and missionary service providers across North America. The result shows that fifty-three of them (38 percent) considered resuming to dispatch mission teams as soon as the pandemic hits downhill in the US. Thirty-nine percent of those

---

13. Bomey, "Secret Vaxxers."

organizations came up with new virtual programs for ministry during the pandemic.[14] Strategic planning and ample training are all the more recommended to send missionaries in the post-pandemic mission. Otherwise, reckless mission trips may bring about more harm than good because there would be still a great portion of the world that isn't COVID-free by then. We must remember that mission is not about the release of our suppressed frustration or proof of my hedonism but about the kingdom of God.[15] Discouragement and ineffectiveness may follow inadequate preparations. Vaccinated missionaries should keep empathy toward unvaccinated local people (not by choice but by lack of supply) when going for overseas missions.

Besides, the hybridity of digital ministry and presence ministry may be a new face of missions in the post-COVID era.[16] I had two or three times more international meetings by virtual means during the pandemic than I had international meetings face to face during the pre-pandemic period. They were as effective as in-person meetings plus cost-effective and time-saving because I already built a personal relationship with most of the delegates in previous in-person encounters. Digital ministry must go hand in hand with presence ministry for the maximum impact.

Even the "going" element of the Great Commission in Matthew 28:19 may need to be contextualized to suit this global change. Rather than terming it only to be typical mobility, which obviously puts limitations both on local and overseas missions during pandemics, we can consider "going" virtually to reach remote regions during travel-restricted pandemics. This strategy can also extend beyond post-pandemic eras for the efficiency of missions. There is certainly merit in going and making disciples of the nations face to face from the grassroots. Yet a prayerful search for reliable local gospel workers (2 Timothy 2:2) in the travel-restricted regions can be an alternative approach. Equipping them virtually and supporting their work (when and where we find it difficult to go ourselves)

---

14. Missio Nexus, "COVID-19 Impact—Fall 2020 Update."
15. Lee, *Disciples of the Nations*, 128–29.
16. Moore, "A Sunday Bummer: Online Preachers Miss the Point."

can be another way to reach the world in both pandemic and post-pandemic seasons.

It is undoubtedly challenging to connect with reliable local people and equip them via virtual means. However, the Holy Spirit can, and does, work through contemporary methods, steps, and principles of missions. Most of all, he can minister to the hearts of local people as we let him through our prayers even from afar. We need to trust in the power of Christ's words to transform people's lives when they're properly imparted in their hearts (Colossians 3:16). Pray that the Holy Spirit will connect you to the right people through the online medium of virtual training, resources, teachings, etc. It is advised to give it a substantial amount of time for interaction and observation to discover proven leadership qualities among your online disciples. Those are readily found in Paul's exhortations in 1 Timothy and Titus. Such a process shouldn't be made in haste. I've witnessed certain organizations offering certificates to the participants of their online short courses and installing them to leadership immediately after the course completion. Putting ill-equipped Christians in leadership and financing their works is risky and should be discouraged. Incomplete preparation of leaders may well cause more damage to other believers in the long run. Even Jesus took three and half years to produce the seasoned Twelve by living with them. It may take longer for us, let alone by virtual means. Please allow the Holy Spirit to draw such quality disciples to you through your prayers and perseverance.

All in all, friendship evangelism or presence evangelism is still the most powerful missions tool and should not be buried by online ministry. Talking to a neighbor on the sidewalk as you park your car on the way back from work can open a door to friendship evangelism. Maybe befriending your neighbors at a garage sale will be another channel. Hearing their stories and helping them out with no strings attached can open their hearts to you and Christ. It was how Christ's followers conducted their presence evangelism in a vibrant birth period of the early church and even in a dark spiritual age of the medieval church period, and it'll be the same in the contemporary church facing the metamodern culture. Online ministry is but a channel through which the body of Christ makes a real connection with the lost world.

MISSIO DEI IN PANDEMIC

I believe God was doing something extraordinary in the context of the *missio Dei* ("God's mission" in Latin) during the COVID-19 pandemic. An expert in turning mourning to dancing and ashes to crown, our God was refining the body of Christ. This God of the second chance was strengthening the call of discipleship both in small groups and families. Many churches suffered from restrictions posed by governments, with limited access to church meetings and religious assemblies. However, most countries have allowed small units of gatherings, like five to ten people (the number could be different depending on the country). That was a perfect opportunity for the church to take advantage of. At EAPTC, we could basically empower home cell group ministries during the pandemic by training key leaders to take care and lead their small groups. They served alongside pastors and church leaders, and in numerous countries we saw small groups covering their communities everywhere. They strategically represented the body of Christ during the pandemic. After the pandemic shrivels up, we're to witness the strengthened body of Christ in churches and denominations. Their spiritual muscles were to be built up and fortified.

Secondly, family lives took on a fresh value. Extended lockdowns at home showed us the blind spots in our family relationships and taught millions how to stick together during difficulties. Many mighty preachers have fallen in the past because, while they were powerfully used by the Lord in public, their home life was somewhat degraded and resulted in some of their children not following Christ in the footsteps of their parents. One unfortunate statistic shows that most of teens who don't share their parent's religious identity are nones with a Christian parent.[17] It was a great chance for Christian leaders to disciple not only their people outside but inside. We learned to make disciples of all nations, beginning with

---

17. Pew Research Center, "Among Teens Who Don't Share Their Parent's Religious Identity, Most Are 'Nones' with a Christian Parent."

the children in our homes. God was turning our attention to refocus on those valuable areas. At the end of the pandemic, we should be able to see the glory of God in the particular area of our life and ministry. Even during the Spanish flu, it was recorded that pastors provided a theological framework for the pandemic as extended Sabbath and a way to disciple one's family.[18]

During a difficult season like a pandemic, family bonding is a powerful mechanism that can hold its members together. After all, missional families are purposeful and affectionate. Family of a missionary is given a chance to enjoy serving as a team in God's work for the nations. Ideal family bonding is built on the foundation of husband-and-wife bonding. Marriage is called to be first a God-serving institution, not a self-serving institution. The latter is only a byproduct of the former. Healthy family bonding begins with a man who pursues his bonding with God and shepherds his family to maturity in Christ, even during the pandemic. The pandemic itself is challenging enough, but being single often makes it even more challenging.[19] For singles who serve in ministry either at home or overseas, it will be wise for them to join or form a community where they feel they belong and go through the crisis together as a team. Such settings will certainly ease up the magnitude of imminent challenges.

Last but not least, a virus that one can't even see with naked eyes taught many people to be vigilant with the hygiene of handwashing and physical distancing from symptomatic individuals. In some parts of the Two-Thirds World where poor hygiene is still widespread, pandemic protocols reminded humanity to pursue a healthy lifestyle. Most of all, it drew people to turn to God and oriented Christians to depend on the Lord for protection. God was truly working through thick and thin of the dark time.

---

18. Nethers, "We've Been Here Before: Lessons from the Church's Responses to the Spanish Flu of 1918–1919."

19. Hoffart et al., "Loneliness and Social Distancing during the COVID-19 Pandemic," 1297.

DEALING WITH UNCERTAINTY IN PANDEMIC

Counseling needs and psychological healing ministry drew the attention of the body of Christ during and beyond the pandemic period. The same goes for missions both at home and abroad. For most leaders, one of the hardest things to deal with during an extended lockdown and quarantine was frustration over an uncertain future and unplannable direction. Leading through the unseen builds in us the characters of true dependency on Christ and humble *followership* as his servant.

> The Lord is my shepherd; I shall not want. He makes me to lie down in green pastures; He leads me beside the still waters. (Psalm 23:1–2)

The famous Psalm 23 depicts the Lord, our Shepherd, leading us to and making us lie down in green pastures. So often, those of us who are not familiar with Israel's geography misunderstand this concept. It was rare for the shepherds to find the plains full of green grass in Israel. Instead, they would lead their flock by grazing the rocky hillsides and tracing a handful of grass near moist rocks. Being biologically near-sighted, the sheep must rely on the leading of shepherds who can see from distance those scattered mouthful-amounts of grasses.

Our Lord, who knows where our provision awaits at every turn, leads us one step at a time in life and ministry. To many Christians today, ministry became more of a lifetime career and less of the call to follow Christ daily. He wants us to depend on him and follow him closely day by day, trusting that he would unmistakably lead us to what we need for now. Green pastures are not everything we need for the rest of our life. This is radically different from the imagery of green pasture in many Westerners' imaginations. However, this is what the Psalmist meant to say when he wrote that "the Lord makes me lie down in green pastures." Green pastures aren't the focal point here. It's the Lord who leads us to green pastures that we should pay attention to. How relevant and applicable concept this is in the midst of the uncertainty of a pandemic!

The Lord is still our Shepherd in the pandemics and epidemics. Christian workers ought to learn to trust that he will lead his sheep even in crisis and help them find their daily green pastures for life and ministry. He'll bless and watch over your family and all your ministry activities as you follow him closely. Jesus is still the Way in the time of uncertainty and at the edge of hope—not programs nor events that can't be carried out during a pandemic. The same Jesus taught his followers to pray for our *daily* bread (Matthew 6:11; Luke 11:3). It is no wonder Christ commanded his disciples twenty-two times in the four Gospels: "Follow me." That applies to both clear season and foggy season.

During the Spanish flu lockdowns, Francis Grimke, a Presbyterian minister, once wrote that he was anxious to get back to the pulpit with his congregants when all his ministry plans seemingly fell out owing to community lockdowns. Yet he later found confidence in God who was in control of everything including pandemics. Grimke confessed that he trusted in the omniscient God who held his future. History confirmed he was right when churches and communities turned to be stronger and better through what they have experienced.[20]

> We can make our own plans, but the Lord gives the right answer. (Proverbs 16:1, NLT)

Pandemic is not just a battle with infectious disease but also with time. Active patience is a lofty virtue we must work on improving to prevail in this difficult time. We may not always know what we're doing in missions. Sometimes we just need to know the One who always knows what he is doing. That is why we should strive to get to know the Lord more every day when we serve in missions.

END-TIME CONSPIRACIES

In the closing remark of this section, we need to be aware of end-time conspiracy theories that usually flame out on a growing apocalypse sentiment during catastrophic eras. At such a calamitous time as a pandemic, we're to keenly cultivate our relationship with

---

20. Grimke, "Some Reflections Growing Out of the Recent Epidemic of Influenza That Afflicted Our City."

the Lord and his unchanging word. It is our Lord Jesus himself who plainly reminded us the following:

> . . . but the end is *still* to come. (Matthew 24:6b, emphasis added)

> All these are the *beginning* of birth pains. (Matthew 24:8, emphasis added)

> And this gospel of the kingdom will be preached in the whole world as a testimony to all nations, *and then the end will come*. (Matthew 24:14, emphasis added)

Matthew 24 and other eschatological Scriptures point the readers to how to behave in the end time, *not* how to calculate the time of Christ's return. The only rightful criterion for the end of the world is when the condition of the gospel of the kingdom being preached in the whole world as a testimony to all nations is met. This makes the task of the mission all the more significant and precious. Upon the basis of the Scriptures, I am assured, it is not the coronavirus (or any other plague, for that matter) that will bring the world to an end. God's eternal word brightly beacons that when the gospel of this kingdom is preached to all the world, only then shall the end come. The church is still the salt and light of the world even amid a gruesome pandemic. Let us never forget what we're called to be in this challenging season.

PART IV

Two Faces Of Suffering

10

Another Face of Persecution

A REAL CHURCH KILLER

> Then you will be handed over to be persecuted and put to death, and you will be hated by all nations because of me. (Matthew 24:9)

Timothy Tennent rebuts the idea that Western Christians "know nothing" or "lack" persecutions. Although persecutions may not come in the West as openly hostile as in parts of the Majority World, they do exist in different forms and are a real and significant part of Christian experiences mutually found elsewhere on earth.[1] Tennent also discourages a belief that persecutions are limited only to chosen martyrs.[2] I echo what Lord Jesus repeatedly said in John 13:16 and 15:20: "Remember what I told you: 'A servant is not greater than his master.' If they persecuted me, they will persecute you also. If they obeyed my teaching, they will obey yours also." He didn't mean to limit his saying only to folks in the early church of the first century or those who live in the gospel-hostile Majority World in the twenty-first century. He meant it for *every* Christian of *every* generation.

1. Tennent, *Invitation to World Mission*, 466.
2. Tennent, *Invitation to World Mission*, 467.

Grenz asserts that every Christian deliberately or implicitly reflects on the content of their beliefs and significance for Christian life.[3] It is through these Christian characteristics that each person represents Christ both individually and corporately. This inborn spiritual nature longed for the need of the Christian community and pulled one another to form a caring and encouraging community that energized the frightened early church believers during persecution. Both near and far, and both then and now, such a belonging sense to the adhesive community has provided vital support for healthy Christian life under persecution. Finding a local church to belong to and a small group to journey together in faith is vitally important to feed vibrant faith. In the same way, the relationship with a sending body plays an indispensable role in keeping missionaries accountable in the field. Here is the hard truth. Anybody, including you and me, can fall, and we need someone else to help guard our spirituality. That is one crucial reason we must pursue a community of mutual accountability.

Mission fields without upfront persecutions don't necessarily mean that they're easy ministry sites and persecution-free settings. Again, 2 Timothy 3:12 stands universal: "In fact, everyone who wants to live a godly life in Christ Jesus will be persecuted." Ironically, persecution never killed the church in history, but prosperity did. Even on the mission fields with no vivid outward persecution, there could be ongoing stresses, corruption to deal with, and continuous discomfort at various degrees everywhere a missionary goes to do his work. In affluent countries with religious freedom, there is another face of persecution—temptation. Persecution and temptation are siblings. In my observations of three decades in ministry serving in three continents, temptations have maligned more Christians in the long run than persecutions.

Forgetting the purpose of God-given prosperity distracts and misleads believers to the stagnation of their missional call. For instance, one of the reasons our faith gets stagnant with growth is that we stop following Christ but try to tame him for us. It should certainly be the other way around. That is a sign of having lost the sense of urgency which the Bible reminds believers not to lose. In

---

3. Grenz, *Theology for the Community of God*, 2.

Matthew 24 and Mark 13, Christ repetitively commands us to stay alert and be on guard in our walk with him.

There is what I call "the danger of safety." Those who practice faith in the free world could fall into an affair with safety even to the point that it keeps them from vigorously engaging in the Great Commission. Besides, our faith life as Western Christians is much swayed by "Christian" moods of impressive music, spectacular lighting, and Bible study programs, etc. Not that I'm neglecting the value of such abundant blessings, they aren't the primary element of Christian discipleship. The primary issue is connected to one's heart, *again*. God should work as powerfully in the hearts of the CAR underground church members who sing unto the Lord with no clap or voice lest they'd be discovered by police to raid and arrest them. Christianity in the West is sometimes referred to as "cross-less Christianity."[4] It is estimated that up to 35 percent of purchased food ends up wasted in the United States.[5] We love (and are almost addicted to) comfort and stuff acquisition. No other country has more garage sales than the United States. Many houses have a surplus of goods at home that is rarely used but simply occupis space. So we wish to get rid of them—to get more stuff.

The Bible lovingly warns us in Deuteronomy 8:12–14 about the risk of the hyper-consumerism mentality:

> Otherwise, when you eat and are satisfied, when you build fine houses and settle down, and when your herds and flocks grow large and your silver and gold increase and all you have is multiplied, then *your heart will become proud and you will forget the Lord your God*, who brought you out of Egypt, out of the land of slavery. (Emphasis added)

Another kind reminder from our Lord is found in Deuteronomy 8:18:

> But remember the Lord your God, for *it is he who gives you the ability to produce wealth*, and so confirms his covenant, which he swore to your ancestors, as it is today. (Emphasis added)

---

4. Borthwick, *Western Christians in Global Mission*, 84.
5. Gallo, "Consumer Food Waste in the United States."

Once again, in Deuteronomy 6:24 we further find God's affectionate exhortation on this issue of hyper-consumerism.

> The Lord commanded us to obey all these decrees and to fear the Lord our God, *so that we might always prosper and be kept alive, as is the case today.* (Emphasis added)

Are we pursuing joy and happiness that comes from having Jesus, the ultimate hope on this side of eternity, regardless of surrounding circumstances? Prosperity and material blessings found around us have been granted to us out of his mercy and favor according to the above Scriptures. Comfort, possessions, and fame may come, stay, and go, but they are never to be our life purpose as Christians. A community sidetracked from God and his principles suffers dire consequences in history over time and place. One sure way to keep ourselves spiritually vigilant is to understand God's heart toward the suffering of his people. Lamentations 3:33 vividly clarifies God's heart in relation to this issue:

> For he [God] does not willingly bring affliction or grief to anyone.

Idolatry is about one's dependency on non-eternal things regardless of space and time. Those things are but short-lived and ever-fluctuating, so the Bible prohibits our worship of them. Eunice, who lived and ministered with me in four different countries, told me one day: "Some people are never rich enough to share while others are never poor enough not to share." I deeply love and appreciate her commitment to things above, not below. I have to admit that it was by God's tender mercy, Eunice's modest lifestyle, and continuous intercession of my ministry partners I've become who I am today. They faithfully kept me on the course of a heavenly nomad lifestyle.

TAKING UP THE CROSS

Erwin McManus lamented that Christianity has moved from a tribe of renegades to a religion of conformists over the past two thousand years.⁶ Jesus said it crystal clear in Matthew 16:24, Mark 8:34, and Luke 9:23: "Take up your cross and follow me." Whatever happened to this highest call of taking up the cross in our Christian life? Christians in the West may not face external persecution to the degree of their counterparts in the CAR but are still commanded by the same Lord to take up the cross and follow him daily. Do we take up the cross when we see a pop-up window on our computer screen that is linked to pornographic sites? Do we stop and ask for God's help and intentionally choose to do the right things when various degrees of temptation to cheat and lie hit us hard at our workplaces during work hours?

Temptation is just the other side of the coin of persecution. Occasionally, both may come together but it is mostly either-or. A North Korean underground church leader who is constantly on the run from police surveillance may be unlikely struggling with the temptation to watch porn. How could he be? His life is in danger, and he has more immediate issues to deal with for survival. On the other hand, a chance of an American family living in New England to meet a mob of Hindus trying to kill them on the way home after Sunday worship at a local church will be slim. Yet, a son or daughter in the family may be struggling with encroaching suicidal thoughts or a clinging porn addiction every night before going to bed. Both challenges are contrasting but quite as real as the other.

That is why Christ wants us to take up the cross and follow him daily, whether we live in North Korea or in North America. One's God-given cross may be different but uniquely legitimate and dearly personal to each and every believer. The cross is the way to overcome the challenge of both persecution and temptation. The message of the cross that the great Son of God sacrificed himself for us tames our bellicose human aptitudes and dissolves selfish attitudes. The love demonstrated through the cross of Christ electrifies those who acknowledge and accept his saving grace. Reprogramming ourselves to trust in Christ's power rather than our own strengths paves a way to confidence and peace in either challenge. If we truly believe in the risen Christ, we can overcome the

---

6. McManus, *The Barbarian Way*, 5.

fear of death and the temptation of sin because the sin—the root cause of both challenges—has been conquered by his resurrection. In his wisdom-packed letter to the Romans, the apostle Paul bounteously narrates our rightful freedom from both challenges gained through the cross of Christ.

There's a vast difference between ministry done based on a transformed worldview and ministry done out of mere obligation. The former is typically accompanied by joy and willing sacrifice, while the latter often drags us just to get the jobs done. With the transformed worldview and dependency on the Holy Spirit, we're empowered to choose to follow Christ every moment in the part of the world either marked by persecution or surrounded by temptation. Christ's followers can find just enough strength for their victory in the message of the cross whether we're suffering for his name in the persecuted world or resisting chronic temptations in the free world.

The ultimate key to victory is to love the Lord with all our heart, soul, and strength. If one loves Christ more than anything, it'll lead him to overcome both fear and temptation exhibited in either circumstance. I remember a story shared by a young seminarian who desperately struggled with porn addiction for years and subsequent despair out of the guilty complex to the point of considering quitting his ministerial training. One day, he was counseled by a wise professor who encouraged him and prayed for him to find a lady to fall in love with rather than to try tirelessly to fight against his porn addiction. Somewhat odd and unsatisfied, the young man left the professor's office and moved on with his life. Years passed by, and the man reached the time of his graduation from seminary. He accidentally bumped into this professor on the road who asked him gently how he was doing with the addiction. The man, surprisingly, answered, "I totally forgot about that. I've not watched porn for years, I just realized." What happened was soon after the counseling he found and fell in love with a girl of his dreams. He helplessly fell in love with this young lady and to please her became his daily focus, which eventually made his porn addiction a thing of forgotten past. They were married soon after graduation and are faithfully serving the Lord in ministry today. Love

Christ. Fall in love with him all over. That'll lead us to the pathway to freedom over both fear and temptation rather than focusing on overcoming often insurmountable challenges.

FOLLOWING THE WAY

> About that time there arose a great disturbance about the Way. (Acts 19:23)

When Paul ministered in Ephesus, there was a great disturbance in the city. The Way of Christ can cause a great disturbance in one's worldview and concept. It did on mine. When this Way saturated my tiny worldview, it realigned my views on finance, education, time, and relationships to the kingdom criteria. The "Way" (ὁδός or *hodos* in Greek) literally means a road, journey, or path. The Way prescribes to its followers the meaning of life, worldview, principles, and priority. It shows how a human being ought to live to enjoy the fullest and most expressive life. It provides purpose, call, and clarity of life regardless of one's environmental circumstances.

This Way is more than dogma. It is actually the person—the person of Jesus Christ. Jesus depicts himself as the Way (again ὁδός or *hodos* in Greek), the truth, and the life in John 14:6. We're called to pursue and follow him. Following Christ is, and should be, therefore the greatest dream every Christian must chase after. This goalpost sets our compass whether we serve Christ in the world of persecution or in the world of temptation. Humanity awaits to come across someone who spreads the aroma of Christ in both worlds.

Our joy is generally based on our environment, comfort, and even comparison. Some people feel blessed by comparing themselves with less fortunate ones around. Yet, the Scripture below reminds us that the reason for our joy must be none other than Christ.

> Though the fig tree does not bud and there are no grapes on the vines, though the olive crop fails and the fields produce no food, though there are no sheep in the pen and no cattle in the stalls, yet *I will rejoice in the Lord, I will be joyful in God my Savior*. The Sovereign Lord is my strength; he makes my feet like the feet of a deer, he

enables me to tread on the heights. (Habakkuk 3:17–19, emphasis added)

Finding joy in Christ alone ensures our triumph over either persecution or temptation. Temptation is but another face of persecution, only more intriguing and magnetic at times. Nonetheless, we can be immune to both fatalities by surrounding ourselves with godly people. As Ecclesiastes 4:12 states, one may be overpowered, but two can stand together, and three or more won't be easily put down. The community of *us* equips the best of *me*. Suffering usually gets lighter when it is handled by the community of us instead of me alone. It is God's design of the church. We'll then be able to stand either in a world of persecution or temptation—or both—to spread Christ's aroma as his irresistible witnesses.

> For we are the aroma of Christ to God among those who are being saved and among those who are perishing. (2 Corinthians 2:15)

11

Mutual Roles of Believers

LIVING LOCALLY, THINKING GLOBALLY

Non-governmental reports, scholarly works, job opportunities, opinion polls, and people's dialogue with others are unprecedentedly shared in the public domain and increasingly voiced via social media.[1] People are taking steps toward becoming more informed global citizens, even more likely so in the post-COVID world. Whether we like it or not, a born-again believer innately possesses a tendency to think globally and develop a global mindset. This tendency gets incubated in us the moment Christ comes into our lives and is at work to change our spiritual DNA from death to life. It is related to the Abrahamic blessing inherent in the hearts of all believers. It's more than enjoying the collection of new visa stamps on our passports and finding ourselves amused at new cultures. We're called to grow global by embracing Christ's worldview of the nations. Borthwick lays out three incredible benefits of pursuing the lifestyle of a global Christian: (1) significant personal growth, (2) an enlarged perspective, and (3) increased witnessing.[2] Culti-

---

1. Rasch, *Global Challenges Facing Post-COVID-19 Governments and Societies*, 6.
2. Borthwick, *How to Be a World-Class Christian*, 149–52.

vating a global mindset is not only beneficial to Christians but is also a Christian responsibility.

While ministering extensively both in the free world and the gospel-restricted world, I've observed the "comparison syndrome" from both sides of the world. Whenever the believers on either side of the world heard about how their counterpart practiced faith, some responded in unhealthy manners. While the majority is inherently busy with their own life or stands aloof from others, some believers in the free world feel either lucky or guilty over their lifestyle. Some feel lucky because they do not face direct harassments like those in the gospel-restricted world. Others feel guilty because they don't feel as committed as their counterpart seemingly with less disturbance to practice their faith. On the other hand, I've also encountered believers in the gospel-restricted world who envied the believers in the free world and even ended up feeling unlucky and grumbling about their circumstances. Eunice used to minister to children of church leaders who work in the CAR and discovered that some of them inwardly hated what their parents do for a living. Several children even hated God who, they presumed, has made them suffer in a world hostile to Christians by situating them there.

Acts 17:26 recalls that it is God who made all the nations from one man, that they should inhabit the whole earth, and that he marked out their appointed times in history and the boundaries of their lands. While it's quite true that our fellow Christians in the CAR do live and work at the risk of constant threats and immediate assaults, one should not underestimate the indirect spiritual attacks their counterpart believers face in the free world, which constantly and gradually ensnare their souls. That is certainly different at least in appearance from persecutions in the CAR but still very real. It is biblical to give extra honor and care to the parts of the body of Christ that have less dignity since we're all put together by God as the body (James 5:11; 1 Corinthians 12:24). However, maybe a healthier (and more biblical) way to face both situations is to seek mutual cooperation out of brotherly appreciation for each other rather than unrealistic comparison and biased expectation. Otherwise, one can be misled to unhealthy fundraising manipulation and others to opportunistic escapism. Both are mutually called by God to faithfully follow Christ and carry the cross in one's given context and contribute toward the Father's global mission. One does so by overcoming temptations they meet on their paths, and the other by overcoming persecutions at hand. Neither one is spiritually superior nor materially compensated. It is just a different calling.

> I say to you that many will come from the *east* and the *west*, and will *take their places* at the feast with Abraham, Isaac and Jacob in the kingdom of heaven. (Matthew 8:11, emphasis added)

WHAT DO WE OWE THE WORLD?

What exactly do we owe the world as believers? Whether we live in a free world or a restricted world, Paul's attitude of "indebtedness" should be reflected in us all. As Paul described himself as a debtor to everyone (Romans 1:14), so are we indebted to the world and to other Christian counterparts. I believe God wants us to consider each other and ponder feasible ways for mutual cooperation as global Christians.

For one, as Western Christians, we do not necessarily care much about the suffering counterpart of the body of Christ unless/until it directly hits us. Otherwise, it usually doesn't get to us to have skin in the game. Some even cynically analyze from "armchair" spectators' perspectives, observing what is happening in far-off nations from the safety of mission offices or seminaries.[3] Granted, we have enough of our own challenges to deal with first. Yet, I'd like to challenge us to enlarge our worldview to see our Father's world, which is unfathomably larger and more collaborative by nature.

The suffering nature of the body of Christ principally lies within our head—Christ. That is why Christ considers the sufferings (either direct persecution or indirect temptation) of Christians as his own. It is no wonder Jesus said to Saul on his way to Damascus, "Why do you persecute *Me*?" (Acts 9:4; 22:7, emphasis

---

3. Greenlee, *Longing for Community*, 230.

added) Before this incident, Saul of Tarsus has never met Jesus personally, but he was persecuting Christ by persecuting his believers.

You may ask, then, "How do I get connected with my suffering counterpart on the other side of the world?" You can begin by praying for them regularly. Open Doors periodically updates a list of the world's most dangerous places to follow Christ.[4] Reading through the related information and praying for persecuted fellow believers on the list will surely widen your worldview to embrace the world which God loves so much that he'd sacrifice his own Son to redeem it. That is one impactful way to connect with the suffering world. Grant and Janice McClung suggest that free Christians pray for their fellow believers in the restricted world (1) sensitively, (2) scripturally, (3) spontaneously, (4) sensibly, (5) systematically, and (6) strategically.[5] Human wills are feeble. They can surely use our prayers to stay strong in the midst of inevitable fires.

> Continue to remember those in prison as if you were together with them in prison, and those who are mistreated as if you yourselves were suffering. (Hebrews 13:3)

At the same time, we ought to rekindle our commitment to suffer for Christ's sake when the temptations *do* come on our ways. In the book *Longing for Community*, David Smith asks Christians in the West this straightforward question:

> We know about the suffering that new believers so often experience, but how much do *we* suffer—we the missionaries, the supporting churches, those who teach and write about these issues?[6]

As prescribed in 1 Peter 2:24, we're healed by Christ's wounds. Wounds of Christ are sufficient enough to bring healing to marred humanity. His wounds can heal individuals and nations. As our Master Jesus did, our own scars and wounds can be used by God to facilitate healing to the world around us. The head suffered, so does the body. The suffering of the head heals others, so can the

---

4. See Open Doors, "2021 World Watch List Report."
5. McClung and McClung, "How to Pray for Persecuted Believers."
6. Greenlee, *Longing for Community*, 232.

suffering of the body. Our wounds develop in us Christlike character and empathy for other hurting ones.

We all can surely work out this issue of empathy toward others. Empathy is a powerful mechanism to bridge with fellow believers in the body. Even the supporting churches and organizations must cultivate this culture of empathy with their missionaries. They should try to feel what their missionaries feel on the field. They should be mindful of what they can and cannot share about the missionary's work and location. They need to constantly review their church/organization websites and social media to maintain the proper security of their missionaries.[7] I trust that Western Christian leaders can be more effective in their global leadership by developing greater empathy to embrace the global body of Christ. Here are some suggestions for that from Mary Ho of All Nations International.[8] Western Christian leaders can:

- Serve in humility with the global church that is now non-Westerners-dominant in the Global South.
- Partner to address the justice and socio-economic issues facing the global church.
- Promote the biblical idea of the kingdom paradigm for holistic community transformation.
- Develop sound theology of suffering and sacrifice.
- Learn from the vigorous faith of those who have suffered for the sake of the gospel.
- Foster the biblical and global theology, missiology, and leadership model relevant to the West and universally.

HARD TEST

The Bible, God's blueprint for the best human life on earth, provides us a bountiful list of advice on how to minister to the world through our suffering. Christ, our head, set an intrinsic example in

---

7. The Evangelical Alliance Mission, "Communication Checklists," 4.
8. Ho, "When Leaders Drink Tea Together," 4–5.

this regard during the days of his flesh. His example beaconed the brightest at the most unlikely moment of his excruciating suffering of the crucifixion. It must have been matchlessly impressive to the centurion who took charge of Jesus' execution. This man has possibly carried out hundreds of crucifixions before. He watched closely—more closely than anyone—the very last hours of our Lord's incarnate life on earth. This cold-hearted soldier saw something different in Jesus' dying moments. Perhaps he might have been initially surprised by the fact Jesus never cursed his cruel accusers, unlike other previous criminals. Later, he could have been moved by Jesus' compassion on the criminal dying next to him, or Jesus' purposeful death expressed in his final exclamation of "It is finished," or mysterious darkness which came over the whole land, or terrifying earthquake which followed Jesus' death, or maybe something else. Whatever warmed his heart during those hours, it must have meant so special to him that he had to confess, "Surely this man was the Son of God!" (Matthew 27:54; Mark 15:39). He likely has sensed that death couldn't handle this Jesus.

I'm more prone to advocate that the centurion's heart was changed by witnessing Jesus' peerless forgiveness, which unprecedentedly stood out among the criminals he has executed by crucifixion in the past.

> Jesus said, "Father, forgive them, for they do not know what they are doing." And they divided up his clothes by casting lots. (Luke 23:34)

Following his flawless example, early church folks imitated his example to do good to their persecutors. It was brightly portrayed in the suffering of the first martyr in the early church: Stephen.

> Then he (Stephen) fell on his knees and cried out, "Lord, do not hold this sin against them." When he had said this, he fell asleep. (Acts 7:60)

Though unnatural and counterintuitive it may seem, our God still calls us to do the same today.

> You have heard that it was said, "Love your neighbor and hate your enemy." But I tell you, love your enemies and

pray for those who persecute you, that you may be children of your Father in heaven. He causes his sun to rise on the evil and the good, and sends rain on the righteous and the unrighteous. (Matthew 5:43–45)

If you come across your enemy's ox or donkey wandering off, be sure to return it. If you see the donkey of someone who hates you fallen down under its load, do not leave it there; be sure you help them with it. (Exodus 23:4–5)

Do not gloat when your enemy falls; when they stumble, do not let your heart rejoice. (Proverbs 24:17)

Do not be overcome by evil, but overcome evil with good. (Romans 12:21)

The list of those seemingly paradoxical verses goes on. As difficult as it may sound to grasp, the Bible calls this hard test of forgiveness a *call*.

Do not repay evil with evil or insult with insult. On the contrary, repay evil with blessing, because to this you were *called* so that you may inherit a blessing. (1 Peter 3:9, emphasis added)

The rationale of this call to love our persecutors is fundamentally based on the fact that our Father loves both the just and unjust.[9]

How precious is your unfailing love, O God! *All* humanity finds shelter in the shadow of your wings. (Psalm 36:7, NLT, emphasis added)

This is exclusively why and where the supernatural power of forgiveness and healing can be manifested on our persecutors and oppressors. If the church fails to exercise forgiveness and reconciliation to those who disagree and repress her, nothing else can replace her to produce genuine peace on earth. History has enough traces of ugly marks that the church left in the world when she forgot this important call. Forgiveness is the foundational fruition

---

9. Carson, *Love in Hard Places*, 15.

of Christian maturity. Christianity was built upon Christ's forgiveness of sinners. Forgiveness releases the forgiver so that he may experience freedom. Forgiveness is, after all, beneficial to the forgiver. It isn't actually for the enemy but the forgiver himself. Paul addresses the Roman Christians and speaks directly to them about the power of forgiveness in Romans 12:20: "you will heap burning coals on the head" of the enemy. This expression refers to an ancient Egyptian custom in which a person who wanted to show public contrition carried a pan of burning coals on his head.[10] Our act of forgiveness may lead our enemy to repentance and, at the same time, mature us by putting trust in the just and righteous Father who is the ultimate judge.

> Do not say, "I'll pay you back for this wrong!" Wait for the Lord, and he will avenge you. (Proverbs 20:22)

Bona fide fruition of Christian ministry won't be seen unless one begins to think eternally. Believers must be free from consequentialism which desires to see the immediate result and fruit of their work. God may allow some people to see them. Nevertheless, many of those who have gone before us did not see them. The great apostle Paul never saw the Roman Empire kneeling before Christ and acknowledging Christianity as the state religion before he went to be with the Lord. He didn't expect that his letters would end up composing nearly one third of the New Testament and that this would make him the author of more books in the Bible than anyone else. He didn't see any of these while on this side of eternity. Being bound by consequentialism may result in exaggeration of the ministry report and brag about one's work, which could be another channel to slip into temptation.

Most of us began to follow Christ and love him just for the pure reason that he loved us first. When Jesus captivated our souls with his Calvary love, his brightest morning lights started to navigate our paths. The new perspective joyously emerged and guided steps of our life. But somewhere along the line, extra reasons might have crept in. Fame, recognition, money, and self-complacency, to

---

10. Kio, "What Does 'You Will Heap Burning Coals upon His Head' Mean in Romans 12:20?" 418–24.

name a few, aren't biblical reasons to work for Christ. Think about it. You didn't have nor care about any of those factors when you first met Christ. You began to follow him because you loved him. We're called to serve him faithfully whether or not we get the opportunity to see the fruit of the hands of our work. This stewardship attitude should be nurtured in us because it'll guide us through persecution and temptation.

> The thoughts of the wicked are an abomination to the Lord.
> But the words of the pure are pleasant. (Proverbs 15:26)

What would the eternal, all-knowing, and all-powerful owner of everything—God—want from mere humans like us? The Bible straightforwardly settles the score on this truth: *He desires to fellowship with his children.* Just as God takes great delight in us and rejoices over us with singing (Zephaniah 3:17), he wants us to be joyful in him just for who he is. Our God wants us to cherish him whether or not there is a financial blessing or circumstantial comfort because he is far greater and more valuable than anything to us.

Of course, we grasp this priceless truth only when the Holy Spirit points us to it and inspires us to take hold of it. Things like fame, recognition, money, and self-complacency may or may not come on our paths. Our good and merciful God will determine to whom such byproducts should go. Yet it really doesn't matter to someone who pursues God. Any discrepancy would be short of the true gospel. Are we allegiant to honor Christ in both big things and small things? Are we faithfully following him on both significant matters and seemingly insignificant matters alike? As near-sighted human beings with a limited projection capability to gauge into the unseen and eternal perspective, we do not always know what is significant or insignificant in his everlasting parameter.

We frequently pray amiss. The question is, do we trust enough in the Father's absolute goodness and flawless sovereignty through which he allows suffering to his children? Faith in the good Father and trust in his perfect heart energize us to move forward to live out the will of God in a full-fledged manner. Just like our spiritual forefathers in Hebrews 11 who have walked before us and left the legacy of faithful discipleship, we can also be willing to suffer persecution and temptation for Christ.

While there are several possible interpretations about the virtue of Abel's sacrifices which made them fairer than Cain's, Hebrew 11:4 points out that it was Abel's faith that made a major difference.

> By *faith* Abel brought God a better offering than Cain did. (Emphasis added)

Even today, sacrifices of life and ministry made in the context of faith please God and bear fruit of eternal value in the end. Those of us who labor in ministry must have faith that the content of our sacrifices in suffering, small and large, seen and unseen, will be used by God to accomplish his purposes in the *missio Dei*. Sacrifices of forgiveness and faithfulness should be solely based on our trust in the eternal God who sees everything beyond our lifetime.

GUARDING THE HEART

> As a face is reflected in water, so the heart reflects the real person. (Proverbs 27:19, NLT)

Thus, we're to always guard our hearts—the motivation of our actions. The Reformers talked about the human status of *Homo Incurvatus in Se* ("a man turned in on himself" in Latin). Some of our Christian activities might have been based on the crooked self-centered nature of men, and it includes even our endurance over persecution and fights against temptation at times. Why are we striving to keep ourselves faithful in this world of endless struggles? Why are we doing what we're doing for the Lord? Where is our heart based? Is it out of our genuine appreciation for Christ's sacrificial love for us and our pure affection toward Christ? Or is there something else mixed in our motivation as men with self-centeredness and infractions? The status of our hearts will determine the eternal value. It is no wonder that the Bible frequently mentions the heart more than any other word except for the names of our Triune God.

> He who forms the hearts of all, who considers everything they do. (Psalm 33:15)

This is another reason that we should strive to stay accountable by watching one another in the body. God originally designed human eyes to see others, not the self. We can see ourselves precisely only with the aids of God's word (James 1:23) and the eyes of others. A lone ranger won't cut it in the face of persecution and temptation. We need one another. All-sharing love and comfort of brothers and sisters in Christ unwaveringly assisted the early Christians to keep their commitment to faith amid fiery persecution. The same goes for today's believers both in the restricted world and free world. Staying vigilantly accountable to God and one another can get us through.

Prayers of fellow believers undergoing suffering are often refined and avail much. James 5:16 confirms that the prayer of a righteous person is powerful and effective. As Andrew Murray testified, the blessing of persevering prayer is unspeakable.[11] Bekele Shanko, founder of the Global Alliance for Church Multiplication, witnessed firsthand how suffering and persecution refined the faith as he served Christ in Ethiopia and other nations through submission and fervent, desperate prayer.[12] One day, I heard that persecuted underground church believers in North Korea regularly intercede for the prosperous mega-churches in South Korea. They were praying for the believers in a free world not to compromise injustice, tolerate sin, be enslaved by love of money, and be corrupted by sexual immorality. I'm sure the believers in a free world can also be benefitted from such persevering prayers.

GRACE OF PRESENCE AND EMPOWERMENT

The Lord's servants cultivate their relationship with the Lord predominantly through prayer. Without prayer, it'll be unlikely for them to be empowered to face temptation or persecution. Prayer enables God's servants to do his will in either challenging setting. After years of international ministry and character-shaping experiences, God revealed to me a secret of this simple truth: The power

---

11. See Murray, *With Christ in the School of Prayer*, lesson 16.
12. Ho, "When Leaders Drink Tea Together," 3.

of God is in the presence of God, and the presence of God is manifested to those who pay the prices.

> But you will receive power when the Holy Spirit comes on you; and you will be my witnesses in Jerusalem, and in all Judea and Samaria, and to the ends of the earth. (Acts 1:8)

This is the last word of Christ recorded in the Bible before he returned to the Father after his incarnate ministry. According to this Scripture, we would receive power as a result of the Holy Spirit coming upon us. Simply put, God's power is found where the Holy Spirit is present. It is in the presence of the Holy Spirit who dwells in a born-again believer. For anyone aspiring to live as a mighty witness for Christ, full of the Holy Spirit and power, he must walk *with* and *in* and *by* the presence of God. Since our God respects our free will, we might want to voluntarily approve his lordship over us and welcome his loving presence in all aspects of our life (although he is already there). The moment when the Holy Spirit comes and empowers us to walk in his wonderful presence and under his direction, the flow of God's power will enable us to be effective witnesses with signs following (Mark 16:20). As a result of following this simple yet profound principle, we can begin to sense God's presence in a way we never dreamed possible. We'll then realize that he longs to be near us more than we long to be near him. However, there are three prices to be paid to live with a conscious awareness of God's presence. Each price begins with the letter *p*:

1. Price of prayer: It's essential to pay the price of prayer to walk in God's presence. The structure of a tabernacle depicted in Hebrews 9 symbolizes the pattern of prayer that draws us near to his presence. The Scripture shows that to reach the Most Holy Place the high priest had to pass the bronze altar representing prayer of repentance, and the laver representing prayer of submission, and finally, the equipment in the Holy Place which represents thanksgiving, praise, and worship. Constant repentance, submission, and thanksgiving in the form of worship keep us near God. It's often easy to talk about prayer but hard to actually spend time doing it. However, it is as plain as it gets: *no prayer, no power.*

2. Price of person: Too often, Christians over-focus on merely one of the millions of beautiful characters of Christ, including the love of Christ, peace of Christ, humility of Christ, the list goes on. What if we adjust our focus fully on the person of Christ who encompasses all of those incalculable merits? Our God described himself as *I am that I am* (Exodus 3:14), and Christ also claimed himself to be *I am* (John 8:58). Our Lord desires to be everything we need. Let us seek Jesus more than we seek merely one of his characters or things we can gain from him. Christ is all of those combined. May our eyes stay on Jesus, and he'll see that our needs are met.

3. Price of piety: In Numbers 6:1–8, we find a vow of separation of a Nazirite—the anointed servants of God with whom God has done great works in the history of Israel. Just as a Nazirite must keep himself holy by abstaining from wine and other fermented drink, by letting no razor be used on his head, and by not going near a dead body, a person who desires God's empowerment should keep himself pure and holy by not touching the other sex apart from the spouse, by not touching God's glory, and by not touching corrupt wealth (love of money). It is crucial to keep ourselves free from an ungodly lifestyle so that God may find us useful and ready for his good works (2 Timothy 2:21). We shouldn't forget that a great many have fallen in the end by failing to pay the price of piety.

> But as for me, it is good to be near God. I have made the Sovereign Lord my refuge; I will tell of all your deeds. (Psalm 73:28)

GRACE OF PATIENCE THROUGH SUFFERING

> For examples of patience in suffering, dear brothers and sisters, look at the prophets who spoke in the name of the Lord. (James 5:10, NLT)

The same God who restored Elijah's diluted sense of the call during his run away from Jezebel's death threat still speaks with gentle whispers to his suffering servants (1 Kings 19:9–18). His first voice to weary Elijah said, "What are you doing here?" and the second voice, "Go back the way you came!" They reveal this timeless truth: the more marred we are, the more we should return to a life of vision. Our intentional obedience to go back to and stay in our original call reproduces energetic spiritual fervor and revitalizes suffering servants.

Proverbs 17:22 talks about a broken spirit that saps a person's strength. Prolonged suffering can surely drain passion out of God's servants. With God's sustaining power and persevering grace, we should endeavor to view the suffering from the eternal perspective and not give up too soon on our ministry efforts. I've witnessed souls turning to the Lord after their loved ones interceded restlessly, waited patiently, and trusted in God's timing for ten years, twenty years, and even after they went to be with the Lord. Time is one of many tools God uses to fulfill his infinite purpose on a finite earth. Unfortunately, many suffering servants wane to tarry up to God's appointed time.

Oversea missionary work is a marathon, not a sprint. Every ministry is. Short-sighted vision and impatient character won't make it. Disciple-making takes a wrestle through time, rightly more so in cross-cultural contexts where cultures and customs differ. The quantity has its value, but the quality should be prioritized in missions. God approves such missionary works and uses them to change the nations.

In the end, it all comes down to the servant's relationship with the Master. Without a doubt, it's the bottom line of every mission, and it leads to the solution for every agony God's servant faces. The Lord's servants should learn to habitually inquire of the Lord on the matters of ministry. The action is derived from humility. It is the prerequisite of servanthood. Samuel the prophet practiced sensing the Lord's voice at a young age and developed a posture of servanthood: "Speak, your servant is listening" (1 Samuel 3:10b). That is the attitude of God's servant who is ready to take on the missional task of this generation. Willingness to sense God's voice and follow his leading, even if it may include discomfort and suffering, will put us on a path to be used by God right at the center of his move. Learning to wait upon the Lord will grant us strength in all circumstances.

> But those who hope in the Lord will renew their strength. (Isaiah 40:31a)

GRACE OF MATURITY THROUGH SUFFERING

Recently, I heard an interview with someone who is directly involved in helping Christians in Afghanistan, where the Taliban has placed a tremendous amount of pressure and hassles on them after they took over the government upon withdrawal of US troops. He asked the audience to exclusively pray for the Afghan Christians to suffer well for the glory of Christ to be manifested to the point that persecutors might discover the hope of eternity from the testimony of those who risk their lives for the gospel.[13] Heartbreaking it was for me to listen to this interview as the man was urging the believers in the West to pray in such a radical way at the impending reality of extreme conditions Afghan Christians faced. This is the global reality today. People are suffering for the sake of Christ and his eternal gospel at this very hour. The apostle Peter's warning still rings a bell today to every suffering servant.

> Be alert and of sober mind. Your enemy the devil prowls around like a roaring lion looking for someone to devour. Resist him, standing firm in the faith, because you know that the family of believers throughout the world is undergoing the same kind of sufferings. And the God of all grace, who called you to his eternal glory in Christ, after you have suffered a little while, will himself restore you and make you strong, firm and steadfast. (1 Peter 5:8–10)

We can't help but discover the blessing of maturity through persecution (or temptation) when we look to the cross. As I mentioned earlier, I've not met anyone yet who is without a problem in years of my ministry both at home and overseas. The above Scripture from Peter's letter specifically guides us through how to cope

---

13. Amundson, "Afghanistan: What's Happening and What's Next?"

with sufferings and difficulties in life. πάσχω (*pasxo* or "suffering" in Greek) in the text originally meant "to suffer evil."[14] The term implies that Christian suffering has a meaning. It has a righteous purpose. That is why the preceding verse of 1 Peter 5:7 decisively encourages those who are under suffering to *cast all their anxiety on Christ*.

Afterward, 1 Peter 5:8–10 continues to articulate the know-hows of lifestyle that enable us to overcome hardships and to go anxiety-free. It teaches us, most of all, to overcome hardships for our own sake. Verse 8 indicates that suffering (1) keeps us spiritually on alert and (2) helps us remain sober-minded. It goes on to remind us in verse 10 that God (1) restores us, (2) makes us strong, (3) makes us firm, and (4) makes us steadfast. We notice the inference here that suffering is somehow utilized by God to aid us in our growth.

Over the years, I've learned of two main ways God grants answers to our prayers uttered while in suffering. They abide by the principles of elimination and elevation. Zechariah 4:7 reads, "What are you, mighty mountain? Before Zerubbabel you will become level ground." There are two ways to turn the troublesome mountains on our paths into level plains. One is to bulldoze and push away the mountain itself. This is likened to the principle of answering prayers through the elimination of the problem. Another way is to climb the mountain and conquer it. Once we conquer the mountain peak, the trouble of climbing the mountain is gone. Discovering that once disturbant and gusty challenges are under our feet from then on, we become relaxed and tolerant. When God answers our prayers, of course, there are times when he takes away the problem we face. However, he sporadically leaves the problem alone and instead pours out an extra measure of his love on his children to pull them up to the level of maturity where the problem becomes no longer problematic to them. This is another dimension of God's answer to our prayers. It is mostly a long cut but often more beneficial to us because it leads us through a maturing process. Even though the same problem still exists around us, it is not a problem to us as before. It is stationed there just to help us

---

14. Skaggs, "The Problem of Suffering: A Response from 1 Peter."

to pray more and grow closer to God. In most cases, problems in Christian life are but uninvited reminders of our need for prayer. This is the principle of answering prayers through elevation. We should not overlook that God substantially uses the latter principle as we mature in our faith. Sufferings we meet on our paths are meant to make us stronger at the end of the roads. It is rather in the unknowable dimension of God's mystery.

I once heard a pastor preaching at a certain church I visited long ago in suburban Washington DC. He described the problems in life as follows: "Problems in our life are the very proof that we're alive. The dead have no problems. Problems soar us up in the faith. Problems close one door but open another. Problems we face remind us of the importance of family. They mature and enlarge our souls. They cultivate our hearts fertile. They keep us from being arrogant by looking only at the harvest of autumn. Problems allow us to learn the secret to radiating the beautiful aroma of faith amid suffering like juniper trees producing an aromatic scent when crushed." Problems and hardships permitted by God to fall on our paths are not to discourage us but rather to boost us toward greater Christian maturity by utilizing them as stepping stones.

The first part of 1 Peter 5:9 goes on to teach us about another rationale of overcoming hardships: "Standing firm in the faith . . ." Again, the apostle Peter exhorts us to overcome hardships for the sake of others. Christians are blessed to bless. The original word for "blessing" in the Bible, both in Hebrew and Greek, implies outward sharing. The term connotes the response toward others rather than myself. The most appropriate description of the biblical concept of blessing is found in Genesis 12:2–3. The proclamation of God's blessing on Abram (and his spiritual descendants, including us) was to make his people into a source of blessing so that peoples of the earth would be blessed through us. Too many times, we merely focus on building our own powerful legacy and making our names great while God's blessing is designed to benefit others through us as a channel.[15] In other words, we ought to seek God's blessing to share with others. Christian students have to study hard to better help others. Christian businessmen need to work hard and make

---

15. Lee, *Disciples of the Nations*, 17–18.

money to better help others. Christian shoemakers ought to make the best shoes possible for others to enjoy comfortable footwear. Ministers must faithfully discharge their ministerial responsibilities to better serve others. It's not just for us to be content and fulfilled. We're called to go further steps. This is the fundamental concept of what it means to be a Christian in this world. Christians are to excel in their occupations so the works of their hands can make a better world around them. That is how the name of our Lord is hallowed on earth as it is in heaven (Matthew 6:9–10; Luke 11:2).

This concept defies the falsified beliefs about Christian giving, commonly amplified by the prosperity gospel. There is an unbiblical error that deliberately makes God a servile banker. Jesus' teaching in Matthew 13 and Mark 4 has been more or less misinterpreted as if God is obliged to multiply the amount of our giving up to thirty times, sixty times, or even a hundred times. This means that my hundred-dollar giving can be potentially returned to me with a minimum of three thousand dollars and a maximum of ten thousand dollars of profit in due time. Our Lord Jesus unfailingly explained the meaning of this parable in Matthew 13:23 and Mark 4:20. Thirty times, sixty times, and a hundred times multiplication is about hearing God's word and putting it into practice to bear fruit. Our obedience to his word can produce multiple impacts to influence our surroundings. There's only one place in the Bible which we can find in reference to the return of our giving. Luke 6:30 tells us to "give and it will be given to us—in a good measure, pressed down, shaken together, running over, and poured into our laps." Strictly interpreting this text under the context, it doesn't apply only to our giving. It means what it clearly says. Whatever we give to others, including, but not limited to, criticism, praise, love, forgiveness, encouragement, and even alms, it'll return to us in a condensed measure. Thus, we ought to be careful with what we give to others in our life. That is the point of the particular Scripture.

We need to definitely and diligently seek the blessing—but with the right motive. The ultimate beneficiary of God's blessing should be others, not us. It fundamentally contrasts with a deceptive boast of our own kindness to other people. Our life purpose as Christians is tectonically set on the worldview not of this world—purposeful living for the blessings of others. Scripture generally confirms that God is glorified by such lives of his people. The biblical faith pursues excellence in our works and lets other people share our God-given blessings.

This selfless attitude motivates us to overcome any hardship that may come about on our paths. The second half of 1 Peter 5:9 affirms that "our brethren in the world suffer the same things." The wound frequently turns into ministry when it is synchronized with God's plan. Those who previously suffered from a major illness usually develop greater empathy toward the sick and are often used by God to effectively administer healing and care. Many of those who experienced poverty in the past end up serving the poor with adequate understanding and compassion toward them. The ones who have tasted failure and setbacks in life can powerfully encourage others in the pit of discouragement with heartfelt concern and authentic humility. The hardships you're going through today may be the preparation for your future service and ministry for others.

> Blessed be the God and Father of our Lord Jesus Christ, the Father of mercies and God of all comfort, who comforts us in all our affliction, so that we may be able to comfort those who are in any affliction, with the comfort with which we ourselves are comforted by God. For as we share abundantly in Christ's sufferings, so through Christ we share abundantly in comfort too. (2 Corinthians 1:3–5, ESV)

Lastly, we ought to overcome hardships for the sake of our God. The first half of 1 Peter 5:10 prompts us to remember that the God of all grace called us to his eternal glory in Christ. The Scripture affirms that for us to get through difficult moments, we must turn our eyes upon God who has shown us his grace and kindness through the sacrifice of Jesus Christ. During trials, we need to fix our eyes on Jesus, the pioneer and perfecter of faith (Hebrews 12:2). The ultimate key to sustaining through our suffering is to embrace the cross of Christ. We cannot complete the talk about suffering apart from the cross of our Lord Jesus. Looking constantly unto the cross and taking heed of its message spring up indefatigable strength in us to move forward through fierce persecution or lingering temptation.

Over the centuries the reality of a cross has been somehow beautified and degenerated. Many today hardly can grasp what the cross and crucifixion were really like, for in most parts of the world this brutal punishment has been abolished for good. The purpose of crucifixion was to provide a notoriously painful, gruesome, and shameful death. Crucifixion was considered a cruel way to die. The nicest form a person could be executed in the Roman empire was beheading and the cruelest form was crucifixion. A common prelude was scourging, which would cause the victim to lose a large amount of blood and approach a state of shock. The prisoner then usually had to carry the horizontal beam to the place of execution, not necessarily the whole cross, often through a town center to receive humiliation and mock from the public. Crucifixion was typically carried out by specialized teams, consisting of a commanding centurion and several soldiers, who were anatomical experts. The victim was usually stripped naked (including the undergarments).[16] The nails were tapered iron spikes approximately five to seven inches (13 to 18 cm) long with a square shaft 3/8 inch (1 cm) across.[17] In popular depictions of the crucifixion, the victim is shown with nails driven straight through the feet and the palms of the hands. However, scientifically speaking, the flesh of the palms can't possibly support the victim's body weight. The nails were most likely inserted just above the wrist, between the two bones of the forearm (the radius and the ulna), or could also be driven through the wrist, in a space between four carpal bones. As some historians have suggested, the Gospel words in the Bible that are translated as "hands" may have in fact included everything below the mid-forearm.[18]

Death could come in hours or days, depending on the health of those crucified and environmental circumstances. One theory holds that the typical cause of death was asphyxiation. When the whole body weight was supported by the stretched arms, the victim would have severe difficulty exhaling, due to hyper-expansion of the lungs. The victim would then have to draw himself up by

---

16. Phelan, *Crucifixion and the Death Cry of Jesus Christ*, 31–50.
17. Israel, *Brooklyn Star*, 241.
18. Barbet, *A Doctor at Calvary*, 97.

his arms or his feet supported by a woodblock. Roman executioners were said to break the victim's legs, after he had hung for some time, to hasten his death. Once deprived of support and unable to lift himself, the victim would die within a few minutes (John 19:31–32). If death did not come from asphyxiation, it could result from several other causes, including physical shock, dehydration, and exhaustion. Crucifixion was only an arbitrary subset of a much wider continuous spectrum of slow and painful execution methods, which included exposure to wild beasts and birds eating up the victim's legs and eyes while hung on a cross. However, the unusual rapidity of Jesus' death (John 19:33) was due to his previous sufferings and his great mental anguish. Jesus died in just about six hours (9:00 am–3:00 pm). He literally died of a broken heart, possibly a ruptured heart, and hence the flowing of blood and water from the wound made by the soldier's spear (John 19:34).[19]

Why did Jesus have to die in such a horrible manner of death? Human ideas and records have very few clues as to why this exceptionally good man had to die by such a cruel execution except for the reasons of jealousy in leadership, groundless suspicion of rebellion, and political scapegoating from the people around him. Yet, the Bible states much clearer clues for the reason of Jesus' death. The Scripture puts it this way to provide the answer to this centuries-old question, which history has constantly tried to answer otherwise. John 3:16 says, "For God so loved the world that he gave his one and only Son [to die on our behalf], that whoever believes in him shall not perish but have eternal life." By dying on the cross, Jesus took our punishment and offered us remission of our sins (2 Corinthians 5:21). Jesus took our sickness and pain and offered us healing and health (1 Peter 2:24; Matthew 8:17). Jesus took our sin and offered us his righteousness (2 Corinthians 5:21). Jesus took our (spiritual) death and offered us his (spiritual) life (Romans 6:23). Jesus took our poverty and offered us abundance (2 Corinthians 8:9). Jesus took our shame and offered us acceptance in God's family (Hebrews 12:2). Jesus took our rejection and offered us a share of his glory (Matthew 27:46). Also, Jesus redeemed

---

19. Strobel, *The Case for Christ*, 289–96.

us from the curse and offered us blessings (Galatians 3:13–14). All in all, Jesus suffered and died for us to be made whole.

The sinless Jesus took our sins on himself (which he never experienced its weight and curse until he voluntarily became the substitutionary sacrifice to atone for our sins). The spiritual horror of sin and subsequential separation from God the Father made him cry out, "My God, my God, why have you forsaken me?" (Matthew 27:46; Mark 15:34). This spiritual element could have been more painful to Jesus than the physical agony of crucifixion. After all, he loved us with a cross, the greatest expression of love through suffering. Our Lord Jesus even refused to take wine mixed with gall (Matthew 27:34), ancient anesthesia to ease the horrific pain of crucifixion which he foreknew. He desired to taste all the agonies of pain that humanity could suffer by choosing to die on that ghastly cross. Where is God when we're in agony, hopelessness, and despair amid rampant sufferings of mankind? He was, is, and will be, right in the depth of our pains and suffering in past, present, and future. This is his message of love which God wants to convey to us through the cross. When we perceive and are persuaded by this message, Christ's love begins to compel us (2 Corinthians 5:14). The cross is the clearest sign of how far God would go to reach us out of his love. Pondering this irresistible love of God in the heart of our suffering can assuredly rescue us from despair and renew the hope in our risen Savior.

One day when my son was sick, I wished if there was any way I could be sick on his behalf. I would be willing to take his place, but I could not. When God saw the sins and misery of the world, he was willing to take our place, and unlike us, he was able to do so, him being the almighty God. The Bible proclaims it is why Jesus died on that horrible cross while he was altogether innocent. Billions of learned and unlearned, rich and poor, men and women, Jews and non-Jews, and many others in history have decided to believe the reason which the Bible points out as the reason of Jesus' death, and they have lived and died content with it.

Our lives have genuine meanings only when they're saturated by Christ's love shown to us with his sacrifice on a cross. The message of the cross gives power to Christ's followers in day-to-day life, no matter how tough and hard their situation turns out to be. The same Christ challenges us further. He says in Luke 9:23, "If anyone would come after me, he must deny himself and take up his cross daily and follow me," and also in Luke 14:27, "Anyone who does not carry his cross and follow me cannot be my disciple." One survey made on the discipleship status of US churches reports that only 1 percent of US pastors responded churches excel in that area.[20] The stat shows how oblivious many of us are about the love of God. The greatest expression of God's love for us is the *cross*.

This is the Christ whom we serve and follow—a suffering servant of sacrifice and Savior of love. Other beliefs in a counterfeit Christ won't just cut it. Five popular counterfeit Christs include: (1) Christ whose sources are different, (2) Christ whose character is different, (3) Christ whose message is different, (4) Christ whose appeal is different, and lastly (5) Christ whose ending is different.[21] In the church's mission to the world, she is called to imitate Christ in his earthly life, his incarnation, his ministry, and his suffering and selfless giving on the cross.[22]

It is at the heart of the message of the cross we discover that God does not owe anyone of us. Free from the entitlement, we should return to the servanthood lifestyle that enables us not only to survive but also thrive in our walk with the Lord in the midst of persecutions and temptations. Jesus came to serve, not to be served (Matthew 20:28; Mark 10:45). We're to model after Jesus with this regard, too (Luke 22:25–27). The more we claim privilege, the less we're like Jesus.[23] Every believer is a servant of God, either clergy or non-clergy, and either male or female. Paul in Romans 1:1 titles himself *a servant of Christ Jesus*. A servant of Christ is a great person because he serves Christ, but a humble person because he is a servant. A person focused on serving Christ will be energized to give his level best at home, work, and ministry—even in the persecution and temptation.

20. Barna Group, "Year in Review: Barna's Top 10 Findings in 2015."
21. White, "5 Counterfeit Christs to Reject."
22. Greenlee, *Longing for Community*, 145.
23. Nieuwhof, "5 Things That Give Pastors a Bad Name with Unchurched People."

Our God is not distant. He is still Immanuel right in the center of our agony, mistreatment, and suffering. God has been in our shoes before. He is closer than we can ever imagine. Suffering servants can always come to find comfort and courage at the foot of the cross because it is where God's love was overwhelmingly portrayed to us all. Just as one MBC shared about his journey of finding and following Christ, our Father God is not distant from his children who are suffering for his name's sake.[24] At the cross, every child of God can find the grace of maturity amid suffering of either persecution or temptation. In the end, both the ones serving Christ under persecution and temptation are equal companions, fellow disciples, and co-servants who serve the King of kings together in his eternal kingdom. First Samuel 30:24 rightfully claims so:

> The share of the man who stayed with the supplies is to be the same as that of him who went down to the battle. All will share alike.

---

24. Ravelo-Hoërson, "The Persecution by Their Muslim Husbands of Female Converts in Cape Town," 373.

12

God's Will be Done on Earth

GOD'S MISSION LIKE A RIVER

> Sometimes you were publicly exposed to insult and persecution; at other times you stood side by side with those who were so treated. You suffered along with those in prison and joyfully accepted the confiscation of your property, because you knew that you yourselves had better and lasting possessions. So do not throw away your confidence; it will be richly rewarded. You need to persevere so that when you have done the will of God, you will receive what he has promised. (Hebrews 10:33-36)

God's love transcends geographical and political borders. His will stretches beyond human understanding and the three-dimensional world we live in. In his omniscient providence, he executes his redemptive plan. From time to time, suffering is utilized by him to aid us in his grand *missio Dei*. Our Father God is aware of and in charge of the suffering of his children as much as he is aware of and in charge of the course of the world mission.

Various opportunities and ideas have been suggested in this book for doing missions in difficult contexts. While most of these suggestions worked effectively in our own field experiences, I'd love to hear from you with different suggestions or altering feedbacks.

This book is by no means designed to provide a perfect formula of missionary methodologies in difficult contexts or a quick solution to the suffering of persecuted churches and Christians. Nor do I believe this book is a pathfinder for everyone to figure out what to do in such settings either. Rather, I wish we'd all get prayerfully drawn one step nearer to God as well as to suffering believers. It is also my prayer that readers in the suffering world be equipped further by the encouragement of God's word and by the gentle reminder that they're not forgotten. Knowing that there are people out there who care may as well serve as a great refreshment to suffering servants on the front line. At the same time, I desire that the readers in the free world get the transplant of God's heart and eyes by embracing the global view of the body of Christ. It shouldn't be taken as someone else's story any longer. It is a story of my family members in God's house.

Moreover, the story is taking place in a parallel dimension, not linear. We're talking about the persecutions and temptations in the *now*, not during Bible times in the Roman Empire or in the distant future. It's happening somewhere at this present moment. Just like babies are continuously born today in this world, new born-again believers keep discovering their calls today in this world. As new believers are added to the kingdom, there are additional persecuted believers even at this hour on the same earth we coexist. Somebody somewhere is struggling and tempted to give up their faith because of fiery oppressions and pressures.

Even while we enjoy the sweet aroma of coffee this morning, some people wake up under daily pressure and oppression. It never dawned on me until I began to encounter them in my own missionary work. Nowadays, I start my mornings with earnest prayer for them. I regularly pray that they will "look to the Lord and his strength" (1 Chronicles 16:11) for their daily trials. I trust God can use my prayer (together with the prayers of thousands of others like you) to encourage that special someone—my fellow suffering servant—by sensing that he/she isn't alone.

It's happening at this moment right now. Maybe it hasn't gotten under our skins, yet we should be aware that it's so real. It is a different type of daily life. We must ask God to imprint his heart and eyes on us to see this. The persecuted local believers in the world need periodical encouragement and comfort by knowing that there is a caring counterpart in the global body of Christ. Believers with freedom of worship need to be mindful of persecuted believers' pain and learn to build up the body of Christ together in the empathetic unity of the Holy Spirit.

I can't help but notice that this book became somewhat sermonized as I've been writing down the pages. However, my initial conviction and inspiration for this book remain the same up to this last chapter. I may not make a huge difference in this world as a result of writing this book, but at least I pray for God to open your heart to see the reality of suffering around us and to increase compassion and love for mistreated and victimized fellow believers of this day and age. God secured my attention, and I grew with my love for Christ and care for other believers in the process of book writing. For where my interest was, there my research also followed. The more I researched, the more I learned. I attempted to share those insights in this book. It is my prayer that readers will unfold their own passion to serve the global church, especially the hurting ones in it. The very fact that you're reading this book is confirmation that you're probably led by the Lord to share the same blessing. When people like you and me increase in number, the body of Christ will be built up more inflexibly.

God's mission is like a river. A river detours, diverges, and converges when its watercourse is blocked. Even when its flow is restricted by a giant challenge of a dam, it quietly keeps multiplying until it finally overflows the dam. It is omnidirectional by nature. It is the same with God's mission. When it faces restrictions, it finds an alternative route to proceed to fulfill God's will on earth. Christian martyrs aren't necessarily fatalists. They would try as much as they could to act wisely and prudently to minister in safety but, at the same time, were willing to submit to God's will even if that means suffering for his name.

However, suffering servants might want to pay attention to the following difference between lament and complaint. I recall Ann Voskamp's remark on this vital topic.

> Lament is a cry of belief in a good God, a God who has
> His ear to our hearts, a God who transfigures the ugly into

beauty. Complaint is the bitter howl of unbelief in any benevolent God in this moment, a distrust in the love-beat of the Father's heart.[1]

What one desperately needs in the midst of suffering is a lament, not a complaint. Lament essentially differs from a complaint. While a complaint is built on one's doubt of God's goodness, lament is about pouring out one's heart to God based on his trust in God's goodness. Lament reaches out to God who knows our hurt and struggle. Lament admits our finite knowledge of the meaning of the present suffering but trusts in the infinite God who knows where we're heading with this suffering. As a tiny babe helplessly and comfortably cries for his need in the mother's bosom, children of God are at liberty to run to the Lord's presence for comfort and mercy. The baby trusts in the mother's capacity to care for him no matter what. He does not doubt that his help is on the way in due time. In the same manner, we can come before a good God with our cry in the midst of pain and also thank him for however much he already gave us. That is a lament. There is a reason that God has put Lamentations in Scripture. We can always go to the Lord and healthily present our lament. Lament before God releases our deepest anxiety and causes the healing of our souls. Undoubtedly, our Lord will be delighted to mend his servants with incomprehensible peace because he promised that his yoke would be easy and his burden light (Matthew 11:30).

PARADOXICAL GRACE

John Bunyan once said, "In times of affliction, we commonly meet with the sweetest experiences of the love of God."[2] As much as we want to deny Bunyan's paramount voice gleaned from twelve years of his imprisonment through which God gave the world the priceless "Pilgrim's Progress" with its over-two-hundred-language translations, history affirms his remark. Most of us connect better with the Lord in suffering. That is a brutal truth. Many of those

---

1. Voskamp, *One Thousand Gifts*, 175.
2. Bunyan, *The Commemorative Edition of the Works of John Bunyan*, 1296.

who underwent suffering ended up confessing that they came forth as gold after trials, echoing the words of Job:

> But he knows the way that I take; when he has tested me,
> I will come forth as gold. (Job 23:10)

The wife of a missionary who was imprisoned and detained in Turkey once testified:

> What would you say to someone who is in a season of darkness or facing persecution? . . . You have to go to God first. You don't go to your Christian friends, your doctor, or your counselor first. Those things are all good, but you have to know to go to God first. And as you partner with him, you will be able to access his resources and make it through.[3]

A revered preacher, Charles Spurgeon, said, "There are some of your graces which would never be discovered if it were not for your trials."[4] Numerous church leaders and members that I encountered during the worldwide COVID-19 crisis attested to this blessing. The dark tunnel of sickness, loss, and lockdown strengthened their faith during the period. Even for my family, it would not have turned out in the way it did if it weren't for the ongoing trial of the pandemic. We were blessed to experience a constant sense of need for dependency on God for protection, God's continuous provision in a predicament, empowered online teaching ministry to an international dimension, and strengthened family relationships, especially with my teenage son, and more. Indeed, God used the crisis of tiresome periods to build in us a more vibrant God-dependent faith and prioritized lifestyle.

GLORY BEARER

> Yet if anyone suffers as a Christian, let him not be ashamed, but let him glorify God in this matter. (1 Peter 4:16, NKJV)

---

3. Galli, *Your Mission Field*, 26.
4. Spurgeon, *Devotional Classics of C. H. Spurgeon*, 18.

Believers are called to bear God's glory in all circumstances (1 Corinthians 11:7). Christians are glory bearers of Christ even in difficult places and circumstances. Living by our life purpose will ubiquitously reveal God's glory in us, through us, and out of us. We bear his glory because we're connected to God, since the source of man was God. Genesis 1 records that when God created vegetation, plants, and trees, he spoke to the land. When God created fish, he spoke to the water in the seas. Just as the land was the source of vegetation, plants, and trees, water in the seas was the source of fish. Yet, it is noticeable that when God created a man, he spoke to none other than himself. Genesis 1:26 states: God said, "Let us make mankind in our image, in our likeness . . ." This is why we need to depend on God to shine his glory through us: because he is the very source of every goodness in us. Fish have their purpose in nature. So do plants. Humans bear God's glory and reveal it the brightest by living according to his purpose, too.

One other noteworthy reality is that men and women are most lively when they learn to seek and trust in God's provision for everything. Again, we learn from Genesis 1 that all beings must be in contact with their sources to survive. Fish must be in contact with water to survive. Plants and trees must be in touch with the soils of the ground to survive. Man can also live the most humane life only when he remains in contact with his source—God. All things in the universe can fulfill their purposes and roles only when they're connected to and remain in contact with their sources. That is why Jeremiah 9:23-24 says, "Let not the wise boast in their wisdom. A warrior should not boast of his bravery. Don't let the rich boast about their wealth. He who boasts, let him boast in this, To know God, and to boast in God." A man is not to boast of his academic achievement, nor his power, nor his wealth, but God who provides us with everything (1 Timothy 6:17) in his rich mercy and abounding grace.

All of us are from the dust of the ground (Genesis 2:7) and sinners doomed to damnation under God's wrath. Yet, God has decided to shower his amazing grace on us and call us his own legitimate children (1 John 3:1). If he chooses to bless us with a free and comfortable life, it is at his disposal and his favor. He alone deserves praise for this mercy. We just shouldn't be entitled to that privilege. Some of our brothers undergo suffering to follow him in certain parts of the world. That's the way they show their faithfulness and fortitude to him, because he is worth it all. Again, he deserves praise for who he is. Our worship and submission are due our God from either side. This is true discipleship.

> "It was for this very reason I came to this hour. Father, glorify your name!" Then a voice came from heaven, "I have glorified it, and will glorify it again." (John 12:27–28)

WORTHY OF THE PRICE TAG

> I urge you to live a life worthy of the calling you have received. (Ephesians 4:1)

When we go to a store and look around, every item has a price tag on it. Its value is determined according to its price tag. The price of the item is set by the manufacturer by considering the procedure of how the product was made and by calculating how much investment has been put into it. If so, how much is the price tag put on your life? This ought to be one of those questions to be answered by your Creator, the God who orchestrates the panorama of your entire life. Undoubtedly, he'll put the price tag on you with this label: "Worth the life of my Son, Jesus." How much does your life cost? We must remember that the life of Jesus Christ, the King of kings and the Lord of lords, was given, sacrificed, and invested in making you be who you are up to this day. Your life is as precious as the life of Jesus Christ. This is exactly why we must live our life on earth worthy of the price tag put on us, no matter how hard it becomes.

Rather than giving up on our faith journey as some people have done in their hardships, we must faithfully live a life worthy of our price tags, not only for ourselves but for the sake of others and the Lord. We shouldn't have any regrets to live as a seed of blessing for the nations. Dynamic love of Christ's cross stirs our hearts and serves as our driving force. First Corinthians 6:19–20 refreshes our memory by saying, "You are not your own; you were bought at a price." The gospel gives us sufficient reasons to keep going while in harsh suffering.

> Since God had planned something better for us so that only together with us would they be made perfect. (Hebrews 11:40)

We can trust and hold on to God even more in difficult times. First Peter 5:10 reminds us that our sufferings are only "temporary" compared to the "eternal" glory into which we'll enter someday. Even if we are presently going through difficult times, we have reason to overcome impending adversities for ourselves, for others, and, above all, for God's glory.

GOD BE GLORIFIED

Elizabeth Elliot, the bereaved wife of venerable missionary Jim Elliot, who was slaughtered by the Huaorani people of Ecuador, wrote in her book *A Chance to Die* about the story of Amy Carmichael, a missionary to India. Elliot testifies in her book about how Carmichael's life inspired her to move on after the loss of her husband. It was the first year of Carmichael's missionary tenure. One day, she was stranded and frustrated by boats that severely delayed her trip. An older missionary couple who was traveling with her calmly reminded young Amy that *God knows all about the boats* and encouraged her to trust in the Lord for his timing. The statement was engraved on Carmichael and served as a telic motto of her missionary life in India.[5] Learning to wait and tarry until God's good time must have kept Elliot on the course of her faithful lifetime service for Christ beyond the loss of her husband.

Richard and Sabina Wurmbrand suffered immensely under communist rule in their country of Romania. They were attending a congress of every Christian denomination which the communist government convened. While cringing bishops and pastors praised communism and sought the coexistence of the church and ideology at the expense of diluted gospel, Richard was prompted by his wife, Sabina, to stand up and proclaim the truth of Christ. He responded

---

5. Elliot, *A Chance to Die*, 78.

that if he did so, she might lose him. Sabina unhesitatingly told her husband, "I don't wish to have a coward as a husband."[6] Richard's boldness to speak the truth at the risk of consequential imprisonment and torture was one thing, but Sabina's determination to live alone in the following years of mistreatment, hunger, and poverty was certainly another dimension of suffering for Christ.

What draws the line between cowardliness and wisdom? The Bible records that Jesus escaped the hostile crowd (Luke 4:30; John 10:39), Paul escaped in a basket (Acts 9:25), and believers except the apostles evacuated Jerusalem (Acts 8:1). One's motivation matters greatly. It is possible that their time hasn't come yet. The fact that Jesus, Paul, and the Jerusalem believers gave their lives without hesitation when they sensed it was time to do so validates this thought. As our Lord Jesus said in Matthew 11:19, wisdom is proved right by her deeds. Whether one acts out of cowardliness or wisdom we may not always know right away because we can't see his heart. In most cases, however, time will tell later and better.

Vision requires a light to see. Christ is our vision and also our light (John 8:12). The closer we walk with Christ, the more vision-fulfilling life we get to live. Getting to know him day by day will lead us to the path of true success because Jesus is the *Way*. Jesus is far bigger than time and history. My achievement, my success, and my life are but a fraction compared to the magnitude of his omnipotence and omniscience perfectly orchestrating the operation of the universe with his eternal dominion. History recognizes you as what you're known for. That is, by your gifting, not by your title. Therefore, faithfulness to the call is a vehicle through which you can make a difference in this world with that gifting. In life, fame and glory are God's domain. God's servants should never mind them. We're simply called to be witnesses of Christ's undeniable and irresistible love for us—not our own corrupt goodness. Should there be any goodness portrayed in us at all, it must be derived from God's goodness infused in us.

What does a God-glorifying mission look like? Dying for Christ is a one-time gift from heaven, yet living faithfully for him day by day takes a persevering grace. We need resilient Christians

---

6. Ludy, *Set-Apart Femininity*, 27.

who can last for a lifetime of faithfulness. Surely we can't do either with our strength. Pride is innate in us all and cannot be dealt with until we look to the Lord, as John Calvin asserted.[7] Amid harsh persecution, our spiritual forefathers showed us what the faith of martyrdom looks like. They continuously chose life in the Holy Spirit and death to the flesh. They lived a down-to-earth life that wasn't alienated from society. Their faith exemplified complete submission to God's will. It may not be easy to fully understand and exercise the ethos and spirituality of martyrdom, but we can start with faithfulness on little things in our daily life. Luke 16:10 confirms that whoever can be trusted with little can also be trusted with much, and whoever is dishonest with little will also be dishonest with much. While the world is indulged in greed and selfishness, such a martyr-like lifestyle shares out of however much we have, sometimes even out of little we have. It reflects a total servant-stewardship lifestyle. It is a lifestyle of giving, from little things to life itself. It's an imitation of the suffering Servant, Jesus the Messiah.[8]

LIVING FOR GOD'S GLORY

God's goodness is based on the promise of his love. God's love is not lovesickness toward the human. It is far more than that. God loves us because he *is* love (1 John 4:8, 16). God's loving nature glorifies his name. Any human suffering for this loving God is also justified in this context. Mankind was created to love and praise him (Isaiah 43:21). It is our chief life purpose. Even our suffering for Christ's name glorifies God in the fullness of time. A man may suffer for the cause of Christ, yet God is not entitled to anything in return. Nevertheless, out of his goodness and mercy, he often rewards his suffering servants and their households.

Some people misunderstand the main purpose of the Christian life. The Christian life isn't just about getting *what I want* by believing in Jesus. We have overwhelming volumes of Christian literature about formulas such as how to increase faith, how to get

---

7. DeYoung, "A Calvin Clarification."
8. Smither, *Christian Martyrdom*, 2.

blessings, how to be healed, and so on. While these can be useful sometimes, our faith isn't centered around formulas. It is primarily about a relationship. We're called to follow invisible Christ and represent him in the visible world. We ought to love him, depend on him, and glorify him in everything we do as believers living on this side of eternity. Glorifying God culminates in a Christian's relationship with Christ. It is the greatest and most ultimate purpose of a believer's life, both in comfort and suffering.

There are three things we might want to consider for God's glory to be manifested more tangibly in our life. First, we can begin to exercise a God-friendly faith in our task management. Prompted by the Holy Spirit, we need to challenge the impossibles and ask for God's help on those tasks. The tasks that are slightly above my best ability to achieve could be attempted in faith and prayer. When the task is obviously beyond my best human capacity, it will surely give God the glory upon achievement. Everyone will acknowledge that it took God's hand on top of my hard work to bring the task to completion. People will confess "God has done it!" and give God the ultimate glory.

A. B. Simpson put it right when he said, "God is not wanting great men, but he is wanting men that will dare to prove the greatness of their God."[9] Young David's advance against Goliath, the experienced giant warrior, perfectly reflected how great his God (not David) was. God has certainly received glory for raising up and using David through this incident (1 Samuel 17:32–37). The body of Christ has room for many more spiritual adventurers who will only glance at the skills they've sharpened but wholly focus on God's ability to achieve great and God-pleasing tasks. Jeremiah 45:5 warns us, "Should you then seek great things for yourself? Seek them not." This doesn't mean that we shouldn't seek great things. Rather, Scripture prohibits seeking great things for ourselves. We can and ought to seek great things for God's glory. We should dream big in God and his ability. That creates an opportunity to exercise a God-friendly faith on the task.

> Then Jesus said, "Did I not tell you that if you believed, you would see the glory of God?" (John 11:40)

---

9. Simpson, *Days of Heaven upon Earth*, 320.

Secondly, we should learn to persevere by faith. Faith is in demand to hold onto the promise and vision God gave us. Some of us put more faith in our chairs than our almighty God. We scarcely doubt whether or not the chair we use every day at work will support our body weight before sitting on it. Most of us just have a simple, doubtless faith in the man-made chair that it will take care of us. What would hinder us in putting our faith in God, who unfathomably shaped and holds this universe, controls our very breath and heartbeat even at this moment, and promises the best things for our life?

Faith and perseverance go hand in hand. Faith enables us to persevere. And when we persevere with faith, it deepens the root of our trust in the Lord and results in the manifestation of his glory. Without developing a deep root, our faith won't be strong enough to endure testing times. We can easily give up in a predicament. It is likened to the seed falling on rocky soil in Jesus' parable.

> The seed falling on rocky ground refers to someone who hears the word and at once receives it with joy. But since they have no root, they last only a short time. When trouble or persecution comes because of the word, they quickly fall away. (Matthew 13:20–21)

James talks about the same in his letter to Jewish Christians scattered outside Israel.

> Perseverance *must finish its work* so that you may be mature and complete, not lacking anything. (James 1:4, emphasis added)

Perseverance ought to be exercised in a healthy manner. We should persevere with prayer. Perseverance without prayer brings no breakthrough. It gets nowhere. When the going gets tough, we must persevere in a way that our spirit, soul, and body are soundly preserved. Otherwise, the tough times can leave in us harmful self-images. Keeping ourselves healthy in spiritual, emotional, and physical status builds a platform to live out as the seed of blessings for others. Faithful endurance for the call of God is compulsory.

Thirdly, we must practice the kingdom lifestyle for the tangible manifestation of God's glory in every aspect. A basic element of the Christian faith advocates that *Christ suffered the death for us* so *we may enjoy life for him*. We live in an era when the family is under attack from various angles. Mending and restoring a marred family has become one of the foremost assignments to enjoy this Christ-purchased life. Family is the smallest building block of God's kingdom manifested on this earth. The pivot of family life is leveraged by the relationship of husband and wife. Christian couples must make efforts to be connected as truly one.

> *Enjoy life with your wife*, whom you love, all the days of this meaningless life that God has given you under the sun—all your meaningless days. For *this is your lot in life* and in your toilsome labor under the sun. (Ecclesiastes 9:9, emphasis added)

The above Scripture reminds every Christian couple that enjoying life together with their spouse is one of the most meaningful merits a man and woman can cherish in life.

> My lover is radiant and ruddy, *outstanding among ten thousand*. (Song of Songs 5:10, emphasis added)

Even if your marriage may not be so perfect at this moment, the above Bible verse recaps that your current spouse is probably the best choice for you. When you're determined to cultivate and work on your marriage based on this encouragement, you're likely on the right track toward enjoying life. Marriage requires more than love. It requires an *expression of love* that your spouse can feel. Most couples love each other, at least in the beginning stage of their marriage. One of the main reasons for frictions comes with communication failure through thick and thin of the marriage. Your love must be *communicated* in the love language of your spouse.[10] Love is not to be explained but to be felt. This is why God gave his Son to mankind to be their sacrifice. It was his ultimate expression of love, although he spoke countless times to people through prophets that he loves them. We could then feel and sense his love to the point to be compelled to respond: "Christ's love compels us . . ." (2 Corinthians 5:14a).

---

10. For more details about love languages, see Chapman, *The Five Love Languages*.

> For God so *loved* the world that he *gave* his one and only Son ... (John 3:16, emphasis added)

Besides, children should obey their parents to manifest God's kingdom and see his glory in family life. Born-again children must remember that God's word promises blessings to kids who possess obedient hearts for parents. Numerous Scriptures proclaim that they'll be blessed and enjoy long life when they honor their father and mother (Exodus 20:12; Deuteronomy 5:16; Matthew 15:4; 19:19; Mark 7:10; 10:19; Luke 18:20; Ephesians 6:2). However, Ephesians 6:1 and Colossians 3:20 teach us three distinctive principles in obeying parents:

> Children, obey your parents in the Lord, for this is right.

> Children, obey your parents in everything, for this pleases the Lord.

- Children need to obey their parents *in the Lord* (only when their words are in accordance with God's word).
- Children need to obey their *parents*, meaning that both their father and mother should be in agreement with their orders to children. Children are under obligation to obey their parents when the word is agreed upon by both father and mother.
- Otherwise, children need to obey their parents *in everything*.

Kingdom lifestyle ought to be exercised in parenting as well should we desire to see God's glory manifested. Christian parents should practice blessing their children, not embittering them (Ephesians 6:4; Colossians 3:21). Parents need to train their children to covet after their parents' blessings whenever they face matters of great importance in life. Authority to bless children is the greatest inheritance that Christian parents should preserve at any cost. Both by words and deeds, our children must be taught to hunger after spiritual blessings from parents, not just financial inheritance from them. More than ever, Christian parents have to be confident themselves of God-given spiritual authority to bless their children. This was the greatness of Jacob. He was a man who solemnly believed in the God-given authority of his parents. It is no wonder God blessed and used this Jacob to carry on the genealogy of the Messiah to bring him into this world.

Should you have any unsaved family members or loved ones, you can be encouraged to keep trusting in the following scriptural promise and persevere for the salvation of your entire family.

> Believe in the Lord Jesus, and you will be saved—you *and your household*. (Acts 16:31, emphasis added)

It would not be wise to intimidate your unbelieving spouse with the pressure of divorce if he/she refuses to go to church with you. With unyielding prayer for your spouse, a Christian wife should keep submitting to her unsaved husband. A Christian husband ought to keep loving and sacrificing for his wife. The Bible promises that the time will come for your spouse. Meantime, you can keep shining the light of the gospel on your spouse and, at the opportune time, be instrumental in leading him/her to Christ. Again, please do not yield to the temptation to say to your spouse that he/she can't come to church until he/she quits smoking, drinking, or doing other ungodly behaviors. If so, your spouse may never get a chance to put his/her foot in the church. Those things will be dealt with when your spouse personally gets to meet Christ.

God is leading us to live out the kingdom lifestyle with words and deeds. This kingdom lifestyle is more than getting from God what I want. It reflects Christ glorified both in my life and death. These are the characteristics of the kingdom life that shines God's glory brighter in every aspect of our lives. The practice of a God-friendly faith and kingdom lifestyle, along with faithful perseverance, will lead us to live ultimately for God's glory.

MY SOURCE OF STRENGTH

Sustaining strength and patient endurance in suffering do not originate from ourselves but from the Lord. It is his goodness and love that enable us to turn our eyes on Jesus and look into his face amid persecution and temptation.

> Surely your goodness and love will follow me *all the days*
> of my life, and I will dwell in the house of the Lord forever.
> (Psalm 23:6, emphasis added)

The Lord is still our Shepherd as we turn to him for our spiritual, emotional, mental, and physical needs in the face of our challenges. We can readily detect God's steadfast faithfulness and feel his caring hands at the very point of our needs as we reach out to him in troubles. The Shepherd and Overseer of our souls (1 Peter 2:25) has his eyes on his servants who are struggling in either world of persecution or temptation. The gentle voice that revitalized Elijah in his despair still brightens the weary souls of suffering servants and shows them the way forward in his eternal word.

> I will instruct you and teach you in the way you should go;
> I will counsel you with my loving eye on you. (Psalm 32:8)

In the essential reunion scene of Jesus with Peter at the Sea of Galilee, Jesus asked the soon-to-be leader of the early church one pivotal question three different times: *Do you love me?* It is intriguing to discover that Peter never said that he loves the Lord in his responses. Instead, he insisted to stress in all his answers: *You know that I love you, Lord* (John 21:15–17). He kept emphasizing the fact that the Lord knows everything, including his weakness and vulnerability. He knew by then living for and even dying for Jesus would be possible only when he put his reliance on Christ's all-knowing, all-sufficient strength and grace. He learned the priceless lesson after his massive failure of denying Jesus three times. Peter couldn't erase from his memory that his exorbitant denial happened only after a few hours from his unwavering self-confidence that he'd never leave Jesus even if all others might do so (Matthew 26:36; Mark 14:31).

God knows all our fears, weaknesses, pains, and sufferings. When the one who knows everything about us puts us where he wants us to be and calls us for the task he wants us to do, he's more than willing and ready to take us through any hardships on the journey. And on that day, whenever it may come about, that we have our final breath on this earth, all our sufferings will be dissolved and agonies melted away. Our Father will welcome us and reward us. All our tears will be wiped away (Revelation 21:4) when we find ourselves in our Father's loving arms which we dearly longed for and finally hear his tender compliment with his ever-loving smile, "Well done, my good and faithful servant" (Matthew 25:21, 23). No true servant of God could ask for more.

Yearning for that moment of eternal reward rejuvenates our every day to keep offering ourselves as a living sacrifice, holy and pleasing to God, on this side of eternity. During the Japanese occupation of Korea in World War II, the colonizers deemed Korean churches to be the greatest obstacle to controlling Korea. They exerted increased pressure on Korean Christians by formally deifying the Japanese emperor and forcing them to conduct mandatory Shinto shrine visits. Many Korean believers chose martyrdom over worship at Shinto shrines, and, as a result, about two hundred churches were closed down. Chu Ki-chol, a Korean minister, was at the forefront of the opposition, and his denunciation of this practice as idolatry led him to frequent imprisonments and tortures. One of the notorious tortures included having Chu walk on a sharp nail board stretched in front of him while scoffing torturers and his congregants watched him to see whether he would denounce Jesus. Before his last arrest, which led to his death in prison, Chu uttered this prayer during his last sermon at his church: "Lord, help me overcome the power of death. Also, help me endure this tedious suffering."[11] Chu chose eternal Christ and his reward over temporary comfort and denouncement of the Lord he loved.

Both in a free world and restricted world, we need more Christians who will live out the faith of martyrs, trusting in the power of resurrection. Faith in the risen Christ, along with clarity of eternal reality, will rekindle a flame of bona fide discipleship in some of the churches today that have become only talkative, quarrelsome, and divisive with no vibrant power of God. Without conviction about resurrection and eternity, Christians remain immature, stubborn, and powerless no matter how long they've been in the church. Without it, our voice is not influential in society because our life doesn't reflect heaven to the world. The life of a

---

11. Chung, "Must Keep Going."

living martyr requires self-denial and a sacrificial mindset which draws supernatural energy from conviction.

The cross was based on Christ's self-denial for the salvation of mankind. Jesus completed his messianic tasks through the cross. He was a kernel of wheat that fell to the ground and died to produce many seeds (John 12:24–26). Let us not forget that Christianity was built on the sacrificial love of Christ, the Son of God. All other human sacrifices will come short of the magnitude and value of Jesus' suffering for mankind. His bountiful love still constrains us to confess, "If we live, we live for the Lord; and if we die, we die for the Lord. So, whether we live or die, we belong to the Lord" (Romans 14:8). The apostle Paul recognized the secret of this powerful living and reminded believers in Philippi, "For to me, to live is Christ and to die is gain" (Philippians 1:21).

If it were not for the hope of eternity through Christ, any Christian suffering will be nonsensical. When we realize that human history revolves around the axis of redemptive history, eternity perspective saturates our souls, and suddenly the present suffering of our persecution and temptation becomes bearable, knowing it has meaning and it is only temporary. Comfortable and safe life may come or stay or go, but it is never the goal nor priority in the life of Christ-followers. Glorifying Christ, sharing him, and following him precedes it all. Here is a billion-dollar question for us to ponder: Is Jesus worth enduring and overcoming all our sufferings and temptations on this side of eternity? Is he to you?

Here is the resounding remark Doug Birdsall made in front of the young emerging mission leaders at the Lausanne 2006 Young Leaders Gathering. The following statement of Birdsall echoes the heart-piercing agenda every Christian must respond to:

> Brothers and sisters, the challenge is before you. I encourage you, I implore you, I admonish you, and I stand with you as you respond to the mission of God in your generation. As you persevere in ministry through the course of your life, the amount of joy you experience in attaining your ultimate destination will be in direct proportion to the degree of difficulty you face in getting there. How will you respond? Will you answer the call for your generation?

> Will you fulfill the purposes of God in your time? Will you achieve greatness in God's kingdom and for his glory? Or will you play it safe? Will you shrink from the challenge? Will you squander or will you seize an opportunity of historic proportion and global magnitude?[12]

The bottom line is, God doesn't owe anything to any of us in history. He's not even obliged to give us his blessings and favors. We should acknowledge that it is exclusively by his lavishing mercy and grace that he pours out his love on us in different forms and capacities in his own sovereignty. We discover at the core of the gospel message that we're all sinners destined for damnation. Remembering the fact that Jesus died for us—sinners—whether we live in a free world or the gospel-hostile world grants us freedom from the unbiblical entitlement mentality. We can unreservedly give all credit to God for his rightful glory. After all, God deserves our best life for his highest glory and splendor.

This God is calling us out today in his highest honor and most prevalent authority: "Whom shall I send? And who will go for us?" (Isaiah 6:8). Who will represent our loving Master and matchless God both in a free world and restricted world? Honorable and imperative tasks of the King's service still beckons us to his vineyard of the world harvest. It will cost us to complete the Great Commission. Suffering in the form of either persecution or temptation may come to meet us on the way. The tasks aren't always safe and comfortable but are worth our life because they hold eternal value.

Life is but short and brief in comparison with eternity awaiting us. Psalm 103:15 likens it to grass and flower that once flourish and are soon gone. However, when you're serving the Lord, life is never dull. Are we pursuing joy and happiness that comes from having Jesus, the ultimate and best hope on this side of eternity, regardless of surrounding circumstances? If your life is after them by following Christ, I believe you're ready for God to use you for his omnidirectional missions, available and suitable to make an impact on this generation. Will you boldly answer this worthy call of the Master today?

---

12. Birdsall, "Serving the Purposes of God in Your Generation."

So if you are suffering in a manner that pleases God, keep on doing what is right, and trust your lives to the God who created you, for he will *never* fail you. (1 Peter 4:19, NLT, emphasis added)

ARE YOU
Called to Go?
Called to Send?
Called to Promote?

God is raising disciples in the nations.
A family that prays for
and supports them in accord
serves a greater family of God.
Your family is a building block
of God's movement.

To learn more about the works
of EAPTC International and
to stand together to complete
the Great Commission,
please visit:

goeaptc.com
eaptc@eaptc.com

Bibliography

Abdallah, Maher. "Six Million Muslims Leaving Islam Every Year in Africa: Interview with Sheikh Ahmad al Katani." *Al Jazeera* 2000.

Amundson, Kurtis. "Afghanistan: What's Happening and What's Next?" *Missio Nexus* September 20, 2021. https://missionexus.org/afghanistan-whats-happening-and-whats-next.

———. "COVID-19 Impact—Fall 2020 Update." *Missio Nexus* November 9, 2020. https://missionexus.org/covid-19-impact-fall-2020-update.

Anderson, David A. *Gracism: The Art of Inclusion*. Westmont, IL: InterVarsity, 2010.

Austen, Lucy S. R. "From Jim Elliot to John Allen Chau: The Missionary-Martyr Dilemma." *Christianity Today* November 28, 2018. https://www.christianitytoday.com/ct/2018/november-web-only/john-allen-chau-jim-elliot-missionary-martyr-dilemma.html.

Barbet, Pierre. *A Doctor at Calvary: The Passion of Our Lord Jesus Christ as Described by a Surgeon*. Harrison, NY: Roman Catholic Books, 1953.

Barna Group. *Beyond Diversity: What the Future of Racial Justice Will Require of American Churches*. Ventura, CA: Barna Group, 2021.

———. "Evangelism Is Most Effective among Kids." October 11, 2004. https://archive.ph/20140523133411/https://www.barna.org/barna-update/article/5-barna-update/196-evangelism-is-most-effective-among-kids.

———. "What Makes an Engaging Witness, as Defined by Gen Z." November 10, 2021. https://www.barna.com/research/gen-z-witness.

———. "Year in Review: Barna's Top 10 Findings in 2015." December 16, 2015. https://www.barna.com/research/year-in-review-barnas-top-10-findings-in-2015.

Beckwith, Clarence A. "The Types of Authority in Christian Belief." *The Harvard Theological Review* 4.2 (1911) 241–52.

Birdsall, Doug. "Serving the Purposes of God in Your Generation." *Lausanne Movement* August 6, 2007. https://www.lausanne.org/content/serving-the-purposes-of-god-in-your-generation.

Bixler, William G. "How the Early Church Viewed Martyrs." *Christianity Today*. https://www.christianitytoday.com/history/issues/issue-27/how-early-church-viewed-martyrs.html.

Blumenstock, James. "Living as Strangers in a Familiar Land." *American Society of Missiology* December 29, 2020. https://asmweb.org/blog-content/living-as-strangers-in-a-familiar-land.

Bodhi, Bhikkhu. *The Noble Eightfold Path: The Way to the End of Suffering*. Kandy, Sri Lanka: Buddhist Publication Society, 1984.

Boer, Harry R. *A Short History of the Early Church*. Grand Rapids, MI: Eerdmans, 2003.

Bomey, Nathan. "Secret Vaxxers: These Americans Are Getting COVID Vaccinations but Not Telling Anyone." *USA Today* September 2, 2021. https://www.usatoday.com/story/money/2021/09/02/covid-vaccines-shots-anti-vaxxer-vaccination-coronavirus/5670276001.

Borthwick, Paul. *How to Be a World-Class Christian: Becoming a Part of God's Global Kingdom*. Downers Grove, IL: InterVarsity, 2009.

———. *Western Christians in Global Mission: What's the Role of the North American Church?* Downers Grove, IL: InterVarsity, 2012.

Bosch, David. *Transforming Mission: Paradigm Shifts in Theology of Mission*. Maryknoll, NY: Orbis, 1996.

Brewster, Dan. "The 4/14 Window: Child Ministries and Mission Strategy." *Transformation* 14.2 (April 1997) 18–21.

Brockman, David R., and Ruben L. F. Habito, eds. *The Gospel among Religions: Christian Ministry, Theology, and Spirituality in a Multifaith World*. Maryknoll, NY: Orbis, 2010.

Bruun, Christer. "The Antonine Plague and the 'Third-century Crisis.'" In *Crises and the Roman Empire*, edited by Olivier Hekster et al., 201–17. Leiden, Netherlands: Brill, 2007.

Bunyan, John. *The Commemorative Edition of the Works of John Bunyan*, vol. 2. London: London Printing and Publishing Company, 1859.

Cameron, Averil. *The Later Roman Empire, AD 284–430*. Cambridge, MA: Harvard University Press, 1993.

Caputo, John D. *More Radical Hermeneutics: On Not Knowing Who We Are*. Bloomington, IN: Indiana University Press, 2000.

———. *What Would Jesus Deconstruct?: The Good News of Postmodernism for the Church*. Ada, MI: Baker Academic, 2007.

Carson, D. A. *Love in Hard Places*. Wheaton, IL: Crossway Books, 2002.

Carson, Kevin. "If It Weren't for Christians, I'd Be a Christian—Gandhi." *Kevin Carson* July 25, 2019. https://kevincarson.com/2019/07/25/if-it-werent-for-christians-id-be-a-christian-gandhi.

Casper, Jayson. "The Best Advice on Engaging Muslims, from Arab Evangelical Scholars." *Christianity Today* April 9, 2021. https://www.christianitytoday.com/ct/2021/april-web-only/christian-muslim-understanding-islam-quran-muhammad-accad.html.

Chalfant, Eric. "Atheism in America." *Oxford Research Encyclopedia of Religion* January 24, 2018. https://oxfordre.com/religion/view/10.1093/acrefore/9780199340378.001.0001/acrefore-9780199340378-e-420.

Chalke, Steve, and Paul Hansford. *The Truth about Suffering: Why Does It Happen?, What Can We Do about It?* Eastbourne, UK: Kingsway, 1996.

Chapian, Marie. *Of Whom the World Was Not Worthy*. Bloomington, MN: Bethany House, 1978.

Chapman, Gary D. *The Five Love Languages: How to Express Heartfelt Commitment to Your Mate*. Chicago, IL: Moody, 1995.

Christianity Today. "The 50 Countries Where It's Most Dangerous to Follow Jesus in 2021." *Christianity Today* January 13, 2021. https://www.christianitytoday.com/news/2021/january/christian-persecution-2021-countries-open-doors-watch-list.html.

Chung, H. J. "Must Keep Going: *100th Anniversary Memorial Church* Sermon Note." http://100church.org/home/board.php?board=cast&page=11&category=3&sort=user_add1&command=body&no=10860&body_only=y&button_view=n.

Cooper, Brent. "'Beyond' Metamodernism." *Medium* April 15, 2017. https://medium.com/the-abs-tract-organization/beyond-metamodernism-c595c6f35379.

Corwin, Gary. "A Humble Appeal to C5/Insider Movement Muslim Ministry Advocates to Consider Ten Questions." *International Journal of Frontier Missiology* 24.1 (Spring 2007) 5–20.

Croft, Richard. "Muslim Background Believers in Bangladesh: The Mainline Church Scene with these New 'Church' Members from Muslim Backgrounds." *Semantic Scholar* April 2014. http://www.stfrancismagazine.info/ja/images/stories/muslim-background-believer-and-the-church-in-bangladesh.pdf.

Darwish, Nonie. *Cruel and Usual Punishment.* Nashville, TN: Thomas Nelson, 2009.

Dey, Pradip Peter, et al. "Knowledge Abstraction Levels." *WSEAS Transactions on Information Science and Applications* 2.4 (2005) 356–59.

DeYoung, Kevin. "A Calvin Clarification." *The Gospel Coalition* January 15, 2010. https://www.thegospelcoalition.org/blogs/kevin-deyoung/a-calvin-clarification.

Donn, Kyle. "The Dangerous Allure of 'Sexy Christianity.'" *Church Leaders* April 24, 2021. https://churchleaders.com/pastors/pastor-articles/171813-radical-christianity-kyle-donn-dangerous-allure-of-sexy-christianity.html.

Douthat, Ross. "Waking Up in 2030." *The New York Times* June 27, 2020. https://www.nytimes.com/2020/06/27/opinion/sunday/us-coronavirus-2030.html.

Dube, Ryan, and Juan Montes. "Group of 16 Americans and a Canadian, Including Five Children, Kidnapped in Haiti." *The Wall Street Journal* October 17, 2021. https://www.wsj.com/articles/group-of-16-americans-and-a-canadian-including-five-children-kidnapped-in-haiti-11634497450.

EBSCO. "Missions and Missionaries Around the World, 1611–1922." *Atla Historical Monographs Collection.* https://www.ebscohost.com/titleLists/h8c-coverage.pdf.

Eby, L. T., E. J. Rhodes, and T. D. Allen. "Definition and Evolution of Mentoring." In *Blackwell Handbook of Mentoring: A Multidisciplinary Approach,* edited by T. D. Allen and L. T. Eby, 7–20. Oxford, UK: Blackwell, 2007.

Elliot, Elisabeth. *A Chance to Die: The Life and Legacy of Amy Carmichael.* Grand Rapids, MI: Revell, 2005.

The Evangelical Alliance Mission. "Communication Checklists." Cautions to Communicate with Missionaries. Villa Park, IL: TEAM Resources, 2016.

Farrokh, Fred. "Perceptions of Muslim Identity: A Case Study among Muslim-born Persons in Metro New York." PhD diss., Assemblies of God Theological Seminary, 2014.

———. "Pursuing Integrated Identity in Christ in Ministry to Muslims." *Training Leaders International.* https://trainingleadersinternational.org/jgc/59/pursuing-integrated-identity-in-christ-in-ministry-to-muslims.

Freinacht, Hanzi. *The Listening Society: A Metamodern Guide to Politics.* Copenhagen, Denmark: Metamoderna ApS, 2017.

Galli, Mark. *Your Mission Field: How Women Are Rethinking Global Gospel Proclamation.* Carol Stream, IL: Christianity Today, 2019.

Gallo, Anthony E. "Consumer Food Waste in the United States." *National Food Review* 11.20 (1980) 13.

Geisler, Norman L., and Ron Rhodes. *Correcting the Cults: Expert Responses to Their Scripture Twisting*. Grand Rapids, MI: Baker Books, 1997.

Gladwell, Malcolm. *Blink: The Power of Thinking without Thinking*. New York: Little, Brown and Co., 2005.

Glasgow, Joshua, et al. *What Is Race?: Four Philosophical Views*. New York: Oxford University Press, 2019.

Gover, Angela R., Shannon B. Harper, and Lynn Langton. "Anti-Asian Hate Crime During the COVID-19 Pandemic: Exploring the Reproduction of Inequality." *American Journal of Criminal Justice* 45 (2020) 647–67.

Greenlee, David. *Longing for Community: Church, Ummah, or Somewhere in Between*. Pasadena, CA: William Carey, 2013.

Grenz, Stanley J. *Theology for the Community of God*. Nashville, TN: Broadman & Holman, 1994.

Grimke, Francis. "Some Reflections Growing Out of the Recent Epidemic of Influenza That Afflicted Our City." *9Marks* March 27, 2020. https://www.9marks.org/article/some-reflections-growing-out-of-the-recent-epidemic-of-influenza-that-afflicted-our-city.

Groothuis, Douglas. *Christian Apologetics: A Comprehensive Case for Biblical Faith*. Westmont, IL: InterVarsity, 2011.

Guo, Philip J., Juho Kim, and Rob Rubin. "How Video Production Affects Student Engagement: An Empirical Study of MOOC Videos." In *Proceedings of the First ACM Conference on Learning @ Scale*, 41–50. ACM Board: Atlanta, 2014.

Hanks, Geoffrey. *Seventy Great Christians: The Story of the Christian Church*. Kaduna, Nigeria: Evangel, 1998.

Hansen, Collin. "Behind Barbed Wire." *Christianity Today* November 10, 2009. https://www.christianitytoday.com/history/2009/november/behind-barbed-wire.html.

Hedges, Chris. *When Atheism Becomes Religion: America's New Fundamentalists*. New York: Simon and Schuster, 2009.

Ho, Mary. "When Leaders Drink Tea Together." *Lausanne Global Analysis* 10.5 (September 2021). https://lausanne.org/lga-04/when-leaders-drink-tea-together.

Hoffart, Asle, Sverre Urnes Johnson, and Omid V. Ebrahimi. "Loneliness and Social Distancing during the COVID-19 Pandemic: Risk Factors and Associations with Psychopathology." *Frontiers in Psychiatry* 11 (2020) 1297. https://www.frontiersin.org/article/10.3389/fpsyt.2020.589127.

Hopkins, Rebecca. "For Expats and Missionaries, COVID-19 Was a Crossroads." *Christianity Today* November 23, 2020. https://www.christianitytoday.com/ct/2020/december/covid19-expats-missionary-international-life-emergency.html.

Hudson, Dale. "Millennials Have Stopped Attending Online Church." *Church Leaders* July 27, 2020. https://churchleaders.com/youth/youth-leaders-articles/379446-millennials-and-online-church-attendance.html.

Ilo, Stan Chu. "Pandemic, Persecution and Poverty: The Trials, Tribulations and Triumphs of God's People in Africa." Paper presented at the Association of Professors of Mission, St. Mary's College, Notre Dame, IN, 2021.

International Christian Concern. "Christian Evangelist Murdered in Southeast Turkey." *Persecution.org* November 20, 2019. https://www.persecution.org/2019/11/20/christian-evangelist-murdered-southeast-turkey.

Israel, Robert. *Brooklyn Star*. Maitland, FL: Xulon Press, 2003.

Johnson, Barry. *Polarity Management: Identifying and Managing Unsolvable Problems*. Amherst, MA: HRD Press, 2014.

Johnson, Jean. "Why We Should Plant Churches as If There Will be a Coup D'état Any Day." *Evangelical Missions Quarterly* 55.1 (2019) 4–6.

Johnson, Joseph. "Worldwide Digital Population as of January 2021." *Statista*. https://www.statista.com/statistics/617136/digitalpopulation-worldwide.

Johnson, Todd M., et al. "Christianity 2018: More African Christians and Counting Martyrs." *International Bulletin of Mission Research* 42.1 (January 2018) 20–28.

Johnstone, Patrick. *The Future of the Global Church: History, Trends and Possibilities*. Downers Grove, IL: InterVarsity, 2014.

Jones, Sophia. "100 Years Ago, 1.5 Million Christian Armenians Were Systematically Killed. Today, It's Still Not A 'Genocide.'" *Huffpost* April 23, 2015. https://www.huffpost.com/entry/armenian-genocide-controversy_n_7121008.

Jørgensen, Jonas Adelin. *Jesus Imandars and Christ Bhaktas: Two Case Studies of Interreligious Hermeneutics and Identity in Global Christianity*. Frankfurt, Germany: Peter Lang, 2008.

Kighoma, Eraston Kambale. *Church and Mission in the Context of War: A Descriptive Missiological Study of the Response of the Baptist Church in Central Africa to the War in Eastern Congo between 1990 and 2011*. Carlisle, UK: Langham Monographs, 2021.

Kio, S. Hre. "What Does 'You Will Heap Burning Coals upon His Head' Mean in Romans 12:20?" *The Bible Translator* 51.4 (October 2000) 418–24.

Koteskey, Ronald L. *Missionaries and Bribes*. Wilmore, KY: GO International, 2012.

Koutselini, Mary. "Towards a Meta-modern Paradigm of Curriculum: Transcendence of a Mistaken Reliance on Theory." *Educational Practice and Theory* 28 (2006) 55–68.

Krishna, Rekha, and Ganesh Mangadu Paramasivam. "Do Mentors Learn by Mentoring Others?" *International Journal of Mentoring and Coaching in Education* 1 (2012) 205–17.

Lamb, Gregory E. "Art of Dying Well; Missions and the Reality of Martyrdom." *Evangelical Missions Quarterly* 55.1 (2019) 43–45.

Lea, Jessica. "How One NY Church Plant Launched March 1 and Did More Than Just Survive 2020." *Church Leaders* December 29, 2020. https://churchleaders.com/news/387640-jason-james-church-plant.html.

———. "Phil Vischer: What Is an Evangelical, Really?" *Church Leaders* July 24, 2020. https://churchleaders.com/news/386846-vischer-what-is-an-evangelical.html.

Lebron, Christopher J. *The Making of Black Lives Matter: A Brief History of an Idea*. New York: Oxford University Press, 2019.

Lee, Paul Sungro. *Disciples of the Nations: Multiplying Disciples and Churches in Global Contexts*. Eugene, OR: Wipf and Stock, 2021.

———. "Impact of Missionary Training on Intercultural Readiness." *Mission Studies* 36.2 (2019) 247–61.

———. *Missionary Candidate Training*. Merrifield, VA: Evangelical Alliance for Preacher Training/Commission, 2008.

Lester, Stan. "Learning for the 21st Century." In *Standards and Schooling in the United States: An Encyclopedia*, edited by Joe L. Kincheloe and Danny K. Weil, 9. Santa Barbara: ABC-Clio, 2001.

Lewis, Rebecca. "Clarifying the Remaining Frontier Mission Task." *International Journal of Frontier Missiology* 35.4 (Winter 2018) 155–68. https://www.ijfm.org/PDFs_IJFM/35_4_PDFs/IJFM_35_4-Lewis.pdf.

Lewis, Richard D. *When Cultures Collide: Leading Across Cultures*. London: Nicholas Brealey, 2005.

Lin, Qianying, et al. "A Conceptual Model for the Coronavirus Disease 2019 (COVID-19) Outbreak in Wuhan, China, with Individual Reaction and Governmental Action." *International Journal of Infectious Diseases* 93 (April 2020) 211–16. https://www.sciencedirect.com/science/article/pii/S120197122030117X.

Lovelace, Berkeley, Jr. "Americans Will Need Masks Indoors as US Heads for 'Dangerous Fall' with Surge in Delta Covid Cases." *CNBC News* July 8, 2021. https://www.cnbc.com/2021/07/08/us-heading-for-dangerous-fall-with-surge-in-delta-covid-cases-and-return-of-indoor-mask-mandates.html.

Lowry, Lindy. "11 Christians Killed Every Day for Their Decision to Follow Jesus." *Open Doors* March 13, 2019. https://www.opendoorsusa.org/christian-persecution/stories/11-christians-killed-every-day-for-their-decision-to-follow-jesus.

———. "Every Day, 8 Christians Killed for Their Decision to Follow Jesus." *Open Doors* January 15, 2020. https://www.opendoorsusa.org/christian-persecution/stories/every-day-8-christians-killed-for-their-decision-to-follow-jesus.

Ludy, Leslie. *Set-Apart Femininity: God's Sacred Intent for Every Young Woman*. Eugene, OR: Harvest House, 2008.

Luther, Martin. "Whether One May Flee from a Deadly Plague." In *Luther's Works, Vol. 43: Devotional Writings II*, edited by Jaroslav Jan Pelikan et al., 113–38. Philadelphia, PA: Fortress, 1999.

Lyotard, Jean-François. *The Postmodern Condition: A Report on Knowledge*. Translated by G. Bennington and B. Massumi. Minneapolis: University of Minnesota Press, 1999.

Manaloto, Emerson T. *Let the Church Meet in Your House!: The Theological Foundation of the New Testament House Church*. Carlisle, UK: Langham, 2019.

Mangalwadi, Vishal. *Truth and Transformation: A Manifesto for Ailing Nations*. Seattle, WA: YWAM, 2009. Kindle.

Mathieson, Chris. "Ramon Llull." *Evangelical Focus* November 27, 2015. https://evangelicalfocus.com/print/1191/Ramon-Llull.

Mathis, David. "Corona Cannot Prevail against Her." *Desiring God* April 2, 2020. https://www.desiringgod.org/articles/corona-cannot-prevail-against-her.

McClung, Grant, and Janice McClung. "How to Pray for Persecuted Believers." *Lausanne World Pulse Archives* 2011. https://lausanneworldpulse.com/perspectives-php/1419/06-2011.

McGrath, Alister. *The Twilight of Atheism: The Rise and Fall of Disbelief in the Modern World*. New York: Crown Publishing Group, 2007.

McGrath, Alister, and Darren C. Marks. *The Blackwell Companion to Protestantism*. Malden, MA: Blackwell, 2004.

McManus, Erwin R. *The Barbarian Way: Unleash the Untamed Faith Within*. Nashville, TN: Thomas Nelson, 2005.

McNeal, Reggie. *The Present Future: Six Tough Questions for the Church*. Hoboken, NJ: John Wiley and Sons, 2009.

Medina, John. *Brain Rules*. Seattle, WA: Pear Press, 2014.

Miller, Duane. "Power, Personalities and Politics: The Growth of Iranian Christianity Since 1979." *Mission Studies* 32 (2015) 66–86.

Miller, Duane, and Patrick Johnstone. "Believers in Christ from a Muslim Background: a Global Census." *Interdisciplinary Journal of Research on Religion* 11.10 (2015) 5–7.
Moore, Ralph. "A Sunday Bummer: Online Preachers Miss the Point." January 2021. https://www.ralphmoore.net/a-sunday-bummer-online-preachers-miss-the-point.
Morris, Benny, and Dror Ze'evi. "When Turkey Destroyed Its Christians." *The Wall Street Journal* May 17, 2019. https://www.wsj.com/articles/when-turkey-destroyed-its-christians-11558109896.
Murray, Andrew. *With Christ in the School of Prayer: 31 Lessons on Effective Prayer*. Bexar County, TX: Bibliotech Press, 2020.
Nethers, Kristine. "We've Been Here Before: Lessons from the Church's Responses to the Spanish Flu of 1918–1919." *The Aquila Report* August 2020. https://theaquilareport.com/weve-been-here-before-lessons-from-the-churchs-responses-to-the-spanish-flu-of-1918-1919.
Nieuwhof, Carey. "5 Things That Give Pastors a Bad Name with Unchurched People." *Church Leaders* November 2, 2015. https://churchleaders.com/outreach-missions/outreach-missions-articles/265372-5-things-that-give-pastors-a-bad-name-with-unchurched-people.html.
———. "10 Things that Demonstrate the World You Grew Up in No Longer Exists." *Carey Nieuwhof* 2017. https://careynieuwhof.com/10-things-that-demonstrate-the-world-you-grew-up-in-no-longer-exists.
Noble, Alan. *Disruptive Witness*. Downers Grove, IL: IVP Books, 2018.
Norman, Les. *A Tree of Life: A Discipleship Manual*. Vitoria, Spain: Editorial Remar, 1997.
Open Doors. "2021 World Watch List Report." https://www.opendoorsusa.org/christian-persecution/world-watch-list.
———. "Brother Andrew Webcast." *YouTube* March 23, 2015. https://youtu.be/KiLslz7ARLw.
———. "North Korea." https://www.opendoorsusa.org/christian-persecution/world-watch-list/north-korea.
———. "Vietnam." https://www.opendoorsuk.org/persecution/world-watch-list/vietnam.
Open Doors International. "Complete World Watch List Methodology." *World Watch Research* November 2021. https://odusa-media.com/2022/01/Complete-WWL-Methodology-November-2021.pdf.
Operation World. "Pray for: India." https://operationworld.org/locations/india.
———. "Pray for: Pakistan." https://operationworld.org/locations/pakistan.
Oppenheimer, Mark. "A Dispute on Using the Koran as a Path to Jesus." *The New York Times* March 12, 2010. https://www.nytimes.com/2010/03/13/us/13beliefs.html.
Pew Research Center. "1. Religious Affiliation among American Adolescents." September 10, 2020. https://www.pewforum.org/2020/09/10/religious-affiliation-among-american-adolescents.
———. "Among Teens Who Don't Share Their Parent's Religious Identity, Most Are 'Nones' with a Christian Parent." September 4, 2020. https://www.pewforum.org/2020/09/10/religious-affiliation-among-american-adolescents/pf_09-10-20_religion-teens-01-1.
Phelan, Geoffrey L. *Crucifixion and the Death Cry of Jesus Christ*. Maitland, FL: Xulon, 2009.

Phelps, Caleb. "How Valuable Is Children's Ministry?" *Pursuing the Pursuer* August 7, 2017. http://www.pursuingthepursuer.org/blog/how-valuable-is-childrens-ministry?.

Pikkert, Pieter. "Protestant Missionaries to the Middle East: Ambassadors of Christ or Culture." PhD diss., University of South Africa, 2006.

Prout, Ebenezer. *The Life of the Rev. John Williams.* New York: Robert Carter and Brothers, 1850.

Pruthi, Raj. *Indian Caste System.* Delhi, India: Discovery Publishing House, 2004.

Rainer, Thom S. "Seven Reasons Your Online Worship Attendance Is Declining." *Church Answers* December 7, 2020. https://churchanswers.com/blog/seven-reasons-your-online-worship-attendance-is-declining.

Rasch, Firend Alan. "Global Challenges Facing Post-COVID-19 Governments and Societies." *International Journal of Business and Management Research* September 9, 2020. https://www.researchgate.net/profile/Al-R-Firend/publication/351249774_Global_Challenges_Facing_Post_COVID-19_Governments_and_Societies_An_Essay/links/608d48efa6fdccaebdfeb180/Global-Challenges-Facing-Post-COVID-19-Governments-and-Societies-An-Essay.pdf.

Ravelo-Hoërson, Nicole. "The Persecution by Their Muslim Husbands of Female Converts in Cape Town: A Case for Mission-shaped Churches and a Missiology of Suffering," *Mission Studies* 34.3 (2017) 369–91.

Reichard, Joshua D. "From Indoctrination to Initiation: A Non-coercive Approach to Faith-learning Integration." *Journal of Education and Christian Belief* 17.2 (2013) 285–99.

Richardson, Rick. *You Found Me: New Research on How Unchurched Nones, Millennials, and Irreligious Are Surprisingly Open to Christian Faith.* Downers Grove, IL: InterVarsity, 2019.

Rievan, Kirst. "In a Pandemic, Should Missionaries Leave or Stay?" *Lausanne Global Analysis* 9.4 (July 2020). https://www.lausanne.org/content/lga/2020-27/in-a-pandemic-should-missionaries-leave-or-stay.

"Segye seongyo gido jemog 27" ["World Mission Prayer Needs No. 27"]. *Korea Research Institute for Mission* July 2021. www.krim.org.

Selvamani, Charles J. "Dalits, Dalit Christians and Dalit Christian Liberation Theology." *CJSelvamani* November 1, 2020. https://cjselvamani.com/dalits-dalit-christians-and-dalit-christian-liberation-theology.

Sherwood, Harriet. "One in Three Christians Face Persecution in Asia, Report Finds." *The Guardian* January 16, 2019. https://www.theguardian.com/world/2019/jan/16/one-in-three-christians-face-persecution-in-asia-report-finds.

Shimron, Yonat. "New Poll Finds Even Religious Americans Feel the Good Vibrations." *Religion News Service* August 29, 2018. https://religionnews.com/2018/08/29/new-poll-finds-even-religious-americans-feel-the-good-vibrations.

Shreve, Kenneth. *Partnership Theology in Creative Access Regions.* Carlisle, UK: Langham, 2017.

Simpson, Albert B. *Days of Heaven upon Earth: A Year Book of Scripture Texts and Living Truths.* New York: Christian Alliance Publishing Company, 1897.

Skaggs, Rebecca. "The Problem of Suffering: A Response from 1 Peter." *Academia Letters* 2021. https://www.academia.edu/52461274/The_Problem_of_Suffering_a_Response_from_1_Peter_.

Smith, Jesse M. "Becoming an Atheist in America: Constructing Identity and Meaning from the Rejection of Theism." *Sociology of Religion* 72.2 (2011) 215–37.

———. "Creating a Godless Community: The Collective Identity Work of Contemporary American Atheists." *Journal for the Scientific Study of Religion* 52.1 (2013) 80–99.

Smither, Edward L. *Christian Martyrdom: A Brief History with Reflections for Today*. Eugene, OR: Cascade, 2020.

Sobo, E. J., Helen Lambert, and Corliss D. Heath. "More Than a Teachable Moment: Black Lives Matter." *Anthropology and Medicine* 27.3 (2020) 243–48.

Spurgeon, Charles Haddon. *Devotional Classics of C. H. Spurgeon*. Mulberry, IN: Sovereign Grace Publishers, 2000.

Strobel, Lee. *The Case for Christ: A Journalist's Personal Investigation of the Evidence for Jesus*. Grand Rapids, MI: Zondervan, 2007.

Sullivan, Missy. "Why Muslims See the Crusades So Differently from Christians." *History* September 3, 2018. https://www.history.com/news/why-muslims-see-the-crusades-so-differently-from-christians.

Susek, Ron. *Firestorm: Preventing and Overcoming Church Conflict*. Grand Rapids, MI: Baker, 1999.

Szmigiera, M. "World Population by Age and Region 2021." *Statista* August 13, 2021. https://www.statista.com/statistics/265759/world-population-by-age-and-region.

Talman, Harley. *Understanding Insider Movements: Disciples of Jesus within Diverse Religious Communities*. Pasadena, CA: William Carey Library, 2015.

Tennent, Timothy C. *Invitation to World Missions: A Trinitarian Missiology for the Twenty-First Century*. Grand Rapids, MI: Kregel Academic, 2010.

Terry, John Mark, et al. *Missiology*. Nashville, TN: Broadman and Holman, 1998.

Travis, John. "The C1 to C6 Spectrum: A Practical Tool for Defining Six Types of 'Christ-Centered Communities' ('C') Found in the Muslim Context." *Evangelical Missions Quarterly* 34.4 (1998) 407–08.

Vermeulen, Timotheus, and Robin Van Den Akker. "Notes on Metamodernism." *Journal of Aesthetics & Culture* 2.1 (2010) 5677.

Vision of Humanity. "Increase in Natural Disasters on a Global Scale by Ten Times." https://www.visionofhumanity.org/global-number-of-natural-disasters-increases-ten-times.

Voskamp, Ann. *One Thousand Gifts: A Dare to Live Fully Right Where You Are*. Nashville, TN: Thomas Nelson, 2011.

Webber, Robert E. *Ancient-future Faith: Rethinking Evangelicalism for a Postmodern World*. Grand Rapids, MI: Baker Books, 2006.

Wells, Samuel. *Incarnational Mission: Being with the World*. Grand Rapids, MI: Eerdmans, 2018.

White, Lesli. "5 Counterfeit Christs to Reject." *Beliefnet*. https://www.beliefnet.com/faiths/christianity/5-counterfeit-christs-to-reject.aspx.

Williams, Kevin. "Politics, the Media and Refining the Notion of Fault: Section 1 of the Compensation Act 2006." *Journal of Personal Injury Law* (2006) 347–54.

Wilson, Billy. *Generation Z: Born for the Storm*. Nashville, TN: Forefront Books, 2021.

Wingfield, Chris. "Ship's Bell, United Kingdom." In *Trophies, Relics and Curios?: Missionary Heritage from Africa and the Pacific*, edited by Karen Jacobs et al., 127–29. Leiden: Sidestone Press, 2015.

Wright, Christopher J. H. *The Mission of God: Unlocking the Bible's Grand Narrative*. Downers Grove, IL: InterVarsity, 2006.

Yancey, George. *Hostile Environment: Understanding and Responding to Anti-Christian Bias*. Westmont, IL: InterVarsity, 2015.

www.ingramcontent.com/pod-product-compliance
Lightning Source LLC
Chambersburg PA
CBHW051058160426
43193CB00010B/1239